The Practice of
SUCCESSFUL
BUSINESS
MANAGEMENT

The Practice of
SUCCESSFUL
BUSINESS
MANAGEMENT

KENNETH WINCKLES

Kogan
Page

First published in Great Britain in 1986
by Kogan Page Ltd, 120 Pentonville Road, London N1 9JN

Reprinted 1986

British Library Cataloguing in Publication Data

Winckles, Kenneth
    The practice of successful business management: a handbook
    for directors and managers.
    1. Management
    I. Title
    658   HD31

    ISBN 1-85091-111-8

Printed and bound in Great Britain
by Billing & Sons Ltd, Worcester

Contents

Appendices

Foreword

by *Sir Peter Parker, MVO*

Anyone who ever worked with Kenneth Winckles will expect a book by him to be like his style of management: and it is so. The grip on reality, the swift seizing of essentials, the direct and human stress on making things happen, a meticulous reliability — all come shining through in this straight-talking, first-rate exposition.

In his introduction Kenneth Winckles talks of the enormous range of management issues that face general managers and the many skills they need if they are to do their job well. This is indeed true; and any one person setting out to write a book on the subject must understand them all in depth. The author of this book is such a man. He has had a distinguished and wonderfully varied career, which equips him to handle the task and to add the authority of real and successful experience to the many examples of management skill and theory which he so accurately describes.

There is something rather daunting about a book on general management. In going for such a target a lesser writer might easily have shattered the confidence of the managers in small and medium-sized companies at whom the book is aimed. The awesome list of things that managers need to know, and the longer and even more formidable catalogue of things that can go wrong, are truly daunting. There is no such problem with this book. The author weaves a cunning network of inter-relations and linkages between the various aspects of management, making a treatment of the subject which is human in scale without losing either depth or detail. He slips from theory to practice in a way that only a master of both can do with ease.

It is all here; from the basics of budgetary control to the refinements of long-range planning, from the management of people to the management of computers, from cash control to performance appraisal.

Yet another management bible some will say. And at first glance it may seem so. What makes *The Practice of Successful Business Management* different is not the list of topics — you have seen them all before — it is the handling of them. The style, authority and succinctness of Kenneth Winckles' statements, the clarity and reality of the examples used and the workmanlike layout have combined to produce a most original exploration of the elusive art of general management. Achieved with less than half the words used in many rival works.

The Practice of Successful Business Management is not a book you will read once and then confine to the bookshelf. It will remain within arm's length of many who read it for a very long time. If copies should appear in the second-hand bookshops of the next century they are going to be well-thumbed and dog-eared.

Preface

Viscount Caldecote, DSC, FEng
Chairman, Investors In Industry Group plc

I am delighted that 3i is sponsoring the publication of this excellent book.

For 3i one of the major deciding factors in investing in a business venture is the skill of the manager or management team. Whatever the product, whatever the business, the managers seeking 3i support must demonstrate their ability to cope with the multitude of business situations which they will face.

This book will help the owners and managers of small and medium-sized businesses to tackle the planning, the people and the problems which are an inevitable part of business life.

We believe that the advice it provides is both prudent and practical and, above all, relevant to modern business management.

Introduction

This book is intended for the general manager, or those aiming to become general managers, of small and medium-sized businesses. And for those who may be called upon to advise them.

Even with that relatively well defined target, the range is wide, whether classified in terms of size or by nature.

Few in the UK have been fortunate enough to have had sound theoretical education to business degree or post-graduate level. Therefore many general managers arrive in their jobs ill-equipped for the many responsibilities they must shoulder and have to learn everything through practical experience. Unfortunately, some aspects may never be properly covered. This is particularly the case as the speed of change accelerates, with the need for periodic retraining throughout the working life. The young manager can count himself lucky if he is working, or has worked, for a good manager, able and willing to guide and teach his subordinate 'on the job'. There is no better way to learn practical management.

The cause of many business failures lies in the lack of knowledge and understanding of how the manager should organise his business and ensure its control. And, whatever else, he must understand the need for, and meaning of, timely, accurate and clear information relating to key activities. It is the basis of sound navigation. I know from firsthand experience that this is not sufficiently appreciated in many smaller businesses: yet resources are more limited and one is frequently working in an environment where there is less room for error. Nor am I sure that many accountants in practice, who are frequently asked to assist, really understand the forward looking role of management accounting in a business.

The range of required skills is wide by any definition. The general manager should not expect to know the answers better than the specialist, but he must understand the principles affecting his job and have enough understanding of his subordinates' problems and tasks to be able to provide effective guidance, and to appreciate the implications of his plans and activities.

In contrast with large businesses, there will almost certainly be less knowledgeable advice available to the general manager of the smaller business. Managers will often be performing more than one task which in some ways makes management of the smaller business more demanding.

In writing this book, I have drawn on my own experience in the management of both large multi-product international business and the smaller business and start-up situations. For the last ten years of active management as an employee, I worked at a senior level in a leading City merchant bank. This varied experience, perhaps relatively unusual, considerably broadened my knowledge of banking, investment and insurance services. It provided a quite different perspective of the business scene.

So far as I know, the references used in this book are accurate at the time of going to print. It will be recognised, however, that the business situation is dynamic: changes in the legal position arise daily from court cases, and new legislation is constantly being enacted. One recent instance is the Companies Act 1985 — a consolidating measure not easily compared with the preceding company legislation.

Finally, I am most grateful to those who have been kind enough to give me their help and advice — including Keith Tuson on taxation, Archie Reid for computers and Alan Preskett for law. Especially do I appreciate the general help and advice given by a long standing business colleague, Len Heath. And, of course, the book would never have seen the light of day were it not for the devoted help of my secretary, Jo Sheridan, and encouraging support from my wife, Peggy, during the many evening hours applied in its preparation.

Kenneth Winckles
February 1986

Chapter 1

Setting the Business Scene

With a view to profit

This book is concerned with activities which are directed at using resources effectively and with a view to profit. Even when profit is not the only aim of the enterprise, as in the case of a social activity or charity, resources are finite and maximum benefit is achieved through their efficient use. Of course, 'benefits' can be judged from different points of view and according to different criteria.

The development of profitable business in free market competitive conditions has a significant built-in regulator for the allocation of resources: the most efficient will survive. And since business activities are directed at satisfying the needs (or perceived needs) of customers, it follows that the wider benefit should be obtained through such a dynamic system of commerce. Unfortunately, a truly free competitive international market is seldom achieved, for various reasons, including national government policies, the restrictive practices of trade unions, and the domination of the market by business operators who protect themselves from competition through sheer size, cartel or other coercive action. It can be said that the results of practices such as these are to the disadvantage of the consumer who might possibly from time to time bring some influence to bear but can never obtain the kind of quick response which would be forthcoming in a competitive market dominated system.

The word 'profit' is an emotive one in some quarters, but, in business, that is the name of the game. We could talk instead of 'added value', that is, the benefit arising from the use of labour to enhance the value of the product or service being offered, but the argument remains the same. Those who propagate the anti-profit view tend to be either ignorant about economics or politically motivated.

Whatever its shortcomings as a measure of performance, the determination of profit is a quite essential requirement for all concerned with the business process. Differences of judgement are legitimate and to be expected, because accounting for a multiplicity of business activities is as much an art as a science. There must therefore be a full disclosure of the basic policies which have been adopted in determination of the profit. Profit, properly determined, reflects economic growth and is therefore an essential element in the creation of national wealth and the source of funds for business development. It also, of course, affects employment prospects.

Because profit is expressed in the common language of money, success in the employment of capital resources can be stated and compared. It is therefore a very important indicator in directing resources to their most effective use.

Through the currency exchange markets, results in one currency can be expressed in another. At the same time, as is well known, the value of a currency can be unstable, frequently (but not exclusively) through the workings of inflation.

Comparisons over a period of time will need adjustment to exclude the inflation factor if they are to be meaningful. The search for a generally acceptable inflation adjustor has been in progress for many years. The fact that, as yet, there has been no consensus does not mean that there is no need for it. Managers must be constantly aware of its erosive and deceptive influence and, one way or another, make allowances for it.

It must not be assumed that accounts are absolutely accurate. They certainly are not. The conventions by which they are prepared need to be understood if they are to be valuable to management (and, of course, others who need them). Their use is essential in the conduct of business; there is no alternative. The general manager must therefore obtain an understanding of the only compass he has by which to navigate his business. This does not come easily to all, and the innumerate manager is at a great disadvantage. My impression is that the average British manager is less numerate than his opposite number in, say, the USA, Japan and Germany.

The fact that the business is small does not obviate the need for good understanding of financial information; indeed, when financial resources are limited, more precise navigation is required if risks are to be kept to an acceptable level.

Identity of objectives

It is essential for those involved in a business project to agree on its objectives. And when the business is established these must be reviewed from time to time.

Two colleagues, who see the development of their business in a similar way, may have significantly different personal circumstances which affect their objectives. For example, a man of 55 and another of 45 are likely to have quite different personal needs on that basis alone. The differences need to be anticipated, discussed and resolved early on if the business is not to run into difficulties.

It is equally important to potential or actual financial participants to understand the purposes of the directors and shareholders. It is a very unusual business indeed which does not need some funding, whether from a bank, a leasing organisation or an investor. Investors in particular want to ascertain, as a matter of prudence and in the light of their own objectives, how and when they can expect to realise their investment. Take, for example, a financial institution with, say, a 20 per cent interest in a private company. It will hope to realise that investment within a reasonable period of time — perhaps five years, perhaps seven. How will that be achieved? Will it involve a sale of the company to another company, or some form of quotation on the Stock Exchange? Will that fit the wishes of the principal management who are quite likely also to be shareholders, possibly controlling ones? Quite likely not. And even if the partners start off with agreed intentions, attitudes often change when the time for sale approaches.

They can also change in midstream. On one occasion I was instrumental in introducing a third party to take a 20 per cent stake in a going concern through the purchase of part of the holdings of two controlling shareholders who wished to enjoy some of the fruits of their labours. Naturally, a new shareholders' agreement was needed when the investment was made. What the vendors had not foreseen or, at least, had tended to ignore at the time the cash was on offer, were the ambitions of the new investor and the more critical probing into the management of the company which would occur in the future. The situation in the boardroom rapidly deteriorated to the evident disadvantage of the company. The problem was only resolved when a method of buying out the new investor was finally arranged.

Or take another case. A rapidly growing technological company intent on Stock Market quotation needed access to additional funding to take care of a much more significant research effort than had originally been anticipated. The funding source turned out to be several US venture capital groups. It was very important to establish in advance that the company could live with the pressures which would inevitably arise when some aggressive investors became involved and that, in particular, the senior management and the technical capability could take the strain.

The first golden rule, therefore, for anybody taking a financial interest in a business is to examine carefully the personal objectives of all concerned in the venture and ensure they are compatible. The second important rule is to consider before entering a commitment how and when it might be possible to get out. This should not imply in any way a lack of confidence. It is just common prudence, particularly in the case of companies which do not have, or may not intend to establish, a market in their securities. It is never easy to realise a minority interest in a private company, and a substantial discount on perceived value is nearly always the price which must be paid at the time of sale.

The kind of business set-up which has been referred to so far is an incorporated company with, in consequence, limited liability for the shareholders. This covers the vast majority of projects. However, there are circumstances when a partnership may be more appropriate, or indeed required because incorporation is not feasible. Although most investors seek sensible capital protection, a partnership may have some individual taxation benefits which are worth consideration in special cases.

What business?

It may be argued in the case of start-ups or small established companies that it is unnecessary for them to define their area of business. But I believe it is necessary to stake out the ground, and, having done so, not to depart from it without the most careful consideration.

It is important because definition of the market-place is the basis of any company's whole marketing approach. Internal management skills may be very satisfactory for one business sector but inappropriate for another.

Consider, for example, an operator of a passenger ship: he has to decide whether he is in the shipping business, the transportation business, the cruise business or the leisure business. Or take a magazine publisher: will he aim to publish essentially trade magazines with consequently short runs and a known market-place; or specialised magazines with a controlled but substantial circulation through a clearly defined distribution system; or will he aim for a wide public distribution through newsagents with all the problems of heavy promotion costs and having to trade through many outlets none of which will guarantee sales? The answers to these questions will point to very different skill and attitude requirements, organisation structure and marketing policies.

It is also useful to establish what business it is *not* intended to pursue. Let us consider a manufacturer of ladders. He is in the ladder business, but is he in the 'access' business or the home improvement business? He may decide that he is in the aluminium ladder business but *not* in the wood ladder business; in the domestic ladder business, but *not* touching the industrial side. The skills and equipment needed and the market implications, when stated in this way, will be evident. The real value of a 'negative' policy, that is one by which you intend not to do this or that, is that it greatly assists decision taking because it requires a positive decision to change the policy. With creative marketing executives it is quite easy to find the company moving down a track it may not have intended to follow. One of the roles of the independent chairman I shall advocate later on is to prevent policy drift.

The business plan

Whether those involved in the business are just using their own money or are seeking the participation of banks and/or other investors, a business plan will be required. In the case of a new business it will scarcely be possible to do anything effective until that has been drawn up. And in the case of a going concern, it will be just as important to prepare a new plan each year.

The business plan will reveal essential financial facts which allow proper consideration to be given to the most appropriate method of financing the business; once the plan is settled, the raising of share capital, loans and banking facilities can go ahead. (The business plan is discussed in detail in Chapter 4.)

Anybody who is approached to invest in a project will want to examine in some detail the objectives and forecasts to satisfy himself that they are sound and reasonable. Forecasts of sales revenues are notoriously difficult to make. Data about the market have to be prepared: this may need formal market research. A separate marketing plan may be needed.

The financial proposals must be soundly based and provide adequate contingency plans. It should be borne in mind that new entrepreneurs tend to be confident people, and their market analyses and sales projections particularly may be over-optimistic.

Even when a satisfactory business plan has been prepared demonstrating how the rewards justify the risks, raising the funds may prove difficult, and it is nearly always advisable to seek professional help. Several different approaches may well be necessary before an acceptable solution emerges. Allow plenty of time for this process; decisions are normally slower than would be liked.

Legal form of business entity

Although it is possible to be in business as a sole trader or partner, the personal risks involved and the limits on financial resources are such that the vast majority of businesses in the UK operate as companies.

The essential feature of the legislation contained in the Companies Acts is the limitation of liability of the proprietors — the shareholders. On the other side, the legislation provides a framework for the protection of creditors, for the conduct of the company and for public disclosure by filing with the Registrar of Companies.

What is frequently not understood is that, when a company is incorporated, it becomes a legal entity quite separate and distinct from the shareholders who own it. The relationship of the shareholders to the company is governed by the Companies Acts themselves and, especially, by two key documents:

The Memorandum of Association
— which specifies the business the company may conduct, the share capital

of the company and a statement to the effect that the liability of share-holders is limited.

The Articles of Association
— which specify the rules and regulations by which the company will be conducted. To assist in their preparation, a standard form of Articles has been included in the Companies (Tables A - F) Regulations 1985. Usually Table A applies except to the extent that the particular Articles of the Company regulate to the contrary.

In order to ensure that due protection is provided for those involved with the company, proposed changes which will have a material effect on the content of the Memorandum or Articles can only be made by the adoption by shareholders with voting rights of a resolution which requires support from 75 per cent of those present and voting at a meeting (or on a poll if demanded) declared to be an extraordinary meeting of which not less than 21 days' notice has been given, and which must set out the proposed resolution. Public knowledge of these and many other matters is ensured by the requirement to register specified information with the Registrar of Companies. The files are open for inspection.

Companies are essentially of two types: 'public' or private. The purpose of the private company is to serve the needs of the majority of smaller and medium-sized businesses. Under current legislation a public company is defined, with the result that any other company is a private company.

A public company is defined as a company limited by shares, being a company:

— the Memorandum of which states that the company is to be a public company, and
— which is registered as a public company under the provisions of the 1985 Act.

These provisions are that:

- the name of the company must end with the words 'public limited company' (or the abbreviation 'plc')
— the Memorandum must be in a prescribed form
— the allotted share capital must have a nominal value of not less than the 'authorised minimum' (currently £50,000)
— the allotted share capital must be at least 25 per cent paid up as to nominal value and 100 per cent paid up as to any share premium
— there must be compliance with various rules to ensure that full value has been given for allotted shares.

Under the 1948 legislation, there was a shareholding limit of 50 people. This is no longer a statutory requirement, but there can be limitations imposed by the Articles. The 1985 Act expressly prohibits the issue to the public of securities (that is, shares or debentures) of private companies limited by shares.

A private company is accorded certain privileges, including:

— it may appoint one director only
— a director holding office for life on 18 July 1945 is not subject to removal under S.303 (a dying breed indeed!)
— a director reaching age 70 since the last annual general meeting may continue in office without resolution
— a period of ten months after the end of the accounting period is allowed

for filing (seven months for plc)
- it may commence trading immediately on incorporation
- the Articles may exclude the issue of new shares on a pre-emptive basis
- the rules regarding permissible distribution and prohibiting loans to directors are applied less strictly
- the company secretary need not be formally qualified.

It is frequently the case that, in addition to the Articles of Association, there will be a separate agreement between the shareholders in a private company. The purpose of this is to establish more precisely the relationships, rights and obligations of shareholders as between themselves.

Because of the nature of the company and its control by a limited number of shareholders whose interrelationship is important, it will be usual either in the Articles or in the shareholders' agreement to regulate the manner in which shares may be transferred. The introduction of an unwanted shareholder can be very disturbing. It is therefore usual to provide, in one form or another, that shares to be offered for sale must first be offered to existing shareholders; the basis for arriving at the transfer price is also usually provided for.

It is clearly not possible in a book of this nature to cover in any depth the contents of UK company legislation. However, there is considerable ignorance about the legal nature of the corporate vehicle through which business is carried on and of the responsibilities of directors. It is important for directors to obtain an understanding of these matters, either by reference to published guidelines or by discussion with a professionally qualified person, such as a lawyer or accountant. Such an understanding is likely to be even more important in the years to come.

Shareholders

The shareholders are the owners of the business. It is they who put up the risk capital for the venture. They are essentially 'first in and last out'. The hoped-for reward for the risks taken is an increasing flow of dividends and increased capital value achieved at some time in the future.

The rights and responsibilities of shareholders are established in the Companies Act 1985, in the Articles of Association and in the shareholders' agreement if there is one.

Since the ordinary shareholders ultimately control the company, the balancing of interests is important. The interests of one or more external financiers may also have to be taken into account: in start-up situations, or early development, those putting up loans or guarantees often wish to have a stake in the success of the venture. It will often be the case that control of the company — ownership of more than 50 per cent of the voting shares — will be an important issue requiring early agreement. Although voting control is secured by more than 50 per cent of the shares in issue, a blocking position can be achieved in practice with a significant minority stake. To be sure of absolute control 75 per cent is necessary, so that resolutions requiring a three-quarters majority are certain of adoption. In private companies the issue of control is frequently the source of considerable negotiation in order to achieve a situation acceptable to those investing in the business.

Share capital can comprise the following different types of share:

— *Ordinary*

Frequently referred to as the 'equity' capital. Voting ordinary shares normally control the business. Ordinary shares benefit from the right to accumulated undistributed profits and other increases in net asset value.

— *Preference*

These carry a preferential fixed dividend right, which accumulates if not paid. Normally if dividends are unpaid for a stated period of time, the preference shareholders are accorded the right to vote. In such a circumstance, the balance of control of the company can be upset.

— *Deferred*

Non-voting and standing after all other shareholders. Most frequently they arise in the course of a capital reconstruction.

More detailed characteristics of shares are set out in Appendix 1.

One of the important powers held by the ordinary shareholders is the appointment — and removal — of directors in accordance with company law and the Articles of Association. These powers are normally exercised at the annual general meeting (AGM) which must be held at least once in every calendar year and not more than 15 months after the date of the preceding AGM. In the case of the first AGM, however, it is sufficient that it is held within 18 months of the date of incorporation.

It may also be the case that the shareholders, by agreement, permit the appointment and replacement of one or more directors by certain of the shareholders to 'represent' their interests. While this right is clearly important, and gives the shareholder some protection, it must be recognised that there can be no right to 'mandate' a director nor to have the extent of a director's shareholding taken into account in votes at directors' meetings: in the final analysis it is his responsibility to ensure that the business is conducted in the best interests of the company as a whole. But many boardroom battles have been fought on this issue.

Directors

In the formulation of a business project, the individuals who agree to come together to form the board of directors are of the greatest importance to the success of the business. And the composition of the board will be looked at very carefully by anybody or any institution approached for funding. This fact cannot be stressed too strongly, and it is demonstrated by the care with which the board is presented when a company seeks a listing on the market.

The board will be scrutinised for:

— integrity
— business acumen, based on previous performance
— balance of skills and experience
— independence of character and view
— motivation
— its chairman
— its chief executive.

All company policies and directions stem from the board. The board must have the ability to work together; to formulate and execute business plans; to appoint (or ensure that those responsible appoint) quality managers; to drive the whole business in the required direction; and to set the tone for the company. Responsibility for success or failure lies at the boardroom door. That is where the buck really does stop.

This area requires the most careful thought at all times, and in Chapter 2 the role of the board is considered in more detail.

Financial sources

With decisions taken on the matters considered in this chapter, it will be possible to develop in sufficient detail a proposal which can be presented to potential sources of finance. Financial institutions are inundated with proposals, so the initial impact of the proposal is important. Every proposal must cover certain key factors, but there is no standard approach. It could be set out in the following order:

- table of contents of the presentation
- definition of terms used
- names of directors with brief details of their qualifications and names of professional advisers
- introduction to, and perhaps also a summary of, the proposal
- history of the business
- summary of the market in which the business intends to operate
- outline of the operation and methods to be followed by the business
- the corporate structure
- management and organisation structure
- financial plan
- use to which proceeds will be applied
- assessment of the risks
- future dividend policy
- plans for listing on the Stock Exchange or Unlisted Securities Market
- proposal to the potential financial source
- list of appendices (in which much of the supporting detail may be included).

The following requirements must be met:

- sufficient total funding to meet the estimated requirements, including a reasonable contingency provision
- a proper relationship of borrowing to shareholders' funds (see pp46 and 178)
- sufficient earnings to make a return on the equity capital an attractive reward for the risks involved.

Chapter 3 provides a summary of the more usual funding sources. There is an almost bewildering availability of institutional sources, as well as a variety of government-backed schemes, mostly providing grants to assist research or development projects, or for the development of export markets.

As the question of borrowing is so complex, it is wise for the board to seek legal and financial advice sooner rather than later if the most appropriate solution is to be found. In the case of government funding a proposal must always be approved before any expenditure has taken place. The choice of method of finance will be influenced by the confidence shown by shareholders putting their own money at risk.

In appropriate cases US venture capital funds may be approached. In general these are aggressive in seeking performance and are most likely to be interested in businesses in the field of technology having, or intending to have, a significant US presence. The venture capital market in the USA is more sophisticated than in the UK. In any case US professional advice will be most valuable.

Apart from the provision of equity financing, some venture capitalists will seek to take options over a part of the existing equity shareholders or an option to acquire new shares issued by the company. This gives them the option to acquire shares at a fixed price, established early in the venture, within an agreed period of time. They therefore do not have to put that element of their investment at risk until the outcome is more certain. Another variation is to attach conversion rights to the whole or a part of the amount lent to the company. This gives the lender the option to apply the loan to the acquisition of equity shares at a stated price and within an agreed time. These options, when exercised, have the effect of diluting the existing shareholders' proportions: consideration must therefore be given, at the time the arrangement is made, as to whether this is an acceptable solution for them.

As has already been stated, financiers will make their judgements according to the perceived quality of the company board and management, and its prospects for continuity. Even if the company is sold to the market, both new investors and the original backers will base their decisions on the same considerations. They will not be interested in a wholesale sell-out by the managers who have built the business, and it can be expected that agreement will be required on this vital issue.

Chapter 2

The Board of Directors and the Control of the Company

Composition of the board

The directors are responsible for the conduct of the business. Their duties are defined by the Companies Act and by case law. While not trustees, their role is similar to that of trustees. They are appointed by the shareholders and, subject to law and the Articles of Association, can be removed by the shareholders.

Their overriding duties are to act in the best interests of the company; not to make private profits from their office; and to avoid conflicts of interest between themselves and the company.

Under certain circumstances they can be held personally liable for their actions. It is the case that directors are often too casual and ill informed about the very real responsibilities and duties which attach to the position. In particular, they carry responsibility for the solvency of their company (that is, the ability of the company to meet its liabilities as they fall due) and can be sued for negligence. Fraud, of course, is a criminal act.

Business is conducted by the directors of the company acting as a board. By law there may not be less than one in a private company. In practice, there are usually at least two. There is no legal upper limit, but most Articles impose one; in any case, too many directors makes the board unwieldy. The Articles establish the quorum for the conduct of business.

A director cannot be mandated to act in accordance with some particular interest although it is frequently the case that some shareholding interest is represented by a certain director, and he will, of course, be well aware of that fact. Those who sit on the board of directors owe their primary allegiance to the company. It follows from this that the appointment of trade union representatives to a UK board of directors presents significant problems; it is difficult to understand how there can be any case for a sectional view at board level: board responsibility is indivisible.

Chairman

The chairman is appointed by the board to preside over it. He may be full-time and perform executive functions in addition to his role as chairman. Or he may be only part-time and non-executive. The relationship between the roles of chairman and managing director varies enormously from company to company and should be the subject of agreement between the directors.

The role of chairman in most companies includes:

- representing and presenting the views of the board to those outside the company – public relations

- organising the business at board meetings
- influencing the composition and organisation of the board and providing leadership to it.

In addition, the chairman is often responsible for:

- shareholder relations
- relationships with financial institutions, particularly at the time of seeking a Market quotation or raising funds
- overall relationships with external professional advisers.

Executive directors

An executive director is a member of the board who performs an executive role in the company in addition to his duty as a director.

This dual role frequently causes confusion. Appointment to the board should be based on ability to contribute to the performance of the board as a whole. Thus, the executive director's responsibilities on the board are quite separate and distinct from his executive function. In the boardroom he must step outside his functional role and contribute to, and carry responsibility for, all decisions of the board. A director acting also as an executive manager is acting under a separate service contract with the company.

The managing director

The board almost invariably appoints one of its directors to be responsible to the board for the overall conduct of the business, subject to the policy of the board. This person may be known as the managing director or the chief executive. Whatever the title, the board must define the duties, responsibilities and limits of authority which the position entails.

The managing director is the principal channel through which the board conducts the firm's business. The appointment (and sometimes removal) of the managing director is therefore crucial. This is one reason to prefer, even in quite small companies, to separate the role of chairman from that of the principal manager. They have different duties, and board meetings are generally more effective if there is an independent chairman. Of course, there are many highly effective companies which have combined the role of chairman and chief executive, but the modern tendency is towards separation.

The principal tasks of the managing director are:

- to implement the policies of the board
- to achieve the objectives agreed with the board
- to recommend policy to the board
- to coordinate and direct the work of the other executive directors
- to ensure the board and, in particular, the non-executive directors are kept properly informed about the progress of the business.

Where the role of managing director is combined with that of chairman, it is clearly a very powerful one. With a separate chairman there is effectively a 'court of appeal' for disputes arising at a senior level. And if there is dissatisfaction with the performance of the managing director, it is far more difficult to apply objective tests and obtain the views of the non-executive directors if the managing director is also the the chairman. The power to bring about change is also seriously limited in such cases because non-executive directors tend to be appointed on the initiative of the chairman himself.

Chairman and managing director must work very closely together, meeting frequently – perhaps daily – so that they are both completely in touch with current events and can discuss them as they happen. With a non-executive chairman the working relationship is likely to be less close, with less frequent meetings and discussions. Whatever the working method, it is important that these two critical people are very much on the same wavelength, leading the team of directors in a constructive way.

Functional directors

Executive directors frequently carry primary responsibility for a functional activity, such as finance, marketing or engineering. It is unusual for them to report directly to the board without close prior consultation with the managing director. The general exception to this is the finance director, because the board as a whole will look to him to ensure that the financial position of the company is properly presented to them and he is frequently required to report separately to the board. This exceptional position can be carried further. American practice favours the appointment of a financial controller whose role is broader than that of finance director in the UK: he presents his own report to the board and is regarded as counterweight to and independent of the managing director; he may express an independent opinion on, for example, the year's financial outcome. In any case, the finance director always works closely with both the chairman and the managing director.

All directors need job descriptions, agreed with the managing director and made available to the board. Job content varies from company to company, but together they should form a team of directors with the skills, attitudes and experience necessary to run a successful business.

Non-executive directors

Those directors who are not performing an executive role in the company are usually referred to as non-executive directors. As directors, of course, they carry the same responsibilities as any other director.

My view is that the appointment of at least two non-executive board members is of considerable benefit to the board as a whole and to the executive directors, in small companies as well as large ones, provided that care is taken in their selection. Non-executive directors must be willing to give the necessary time to the task, to obtain a reasonably detailed knowledge of the business and to be properly informed on a regular basis. They can be of special value in board subcommittee work, for example in connection with audit and employment policy matters. Non-executive directors frequently chair subcommittees.

Their value lies essentially in their independence, without which they have no place on the board. In addition to this they should bring to the board a new and broader perspective, and they should be capable of judging the performance of executive directors. They must have integrity and a willingness to express opinions which may not necessarily be welcome to all other members.

The chairman has a special relationship with non-executive directors, often asking them to express an opinion about external matters likely to affect the company. If questions arise about the composition of the board, the chairman will seek sound independent advice from the non-executive directors.

Carefully selected non-executive directors enhance the quality of debate at board level and contribute to the performance of the company.

Subcommittees

Subcommittees of the board are frequently used, either on a permanent or project basis. Subcommittees are effectively assigned the powers of the board, although it is usual for the board to establish at the very beginning their terms of reference.

A permanent subcommittee is often formed to deal with employment matters, including most aspects of the company personnel policies, review of executive remuneration packages and pension policies; it might also oversee the use of performance appraisal and psychological testing procedures within the company.

The audit subcommittee is becoming more common as a permanent feature in UK companies; it provides an independent review of the financial results and improves liaison with the external auditors.

Subcommittees are not a method of ducking difficult board issues.

Company secretary

Every company must, by law, have a secretary. He is not usually a director as well, except in companies with a sole director. The position of secretary carries considerable responsibility; he is frequently required to advise the board on the legal implications of a proposed course of action.

The secretary always reports to the chairman, although his responsibility is to the board as a whole. His precise responsibilities depend on the structure of the board, the skills of its members and the size of the company. In small companies, the position may be held by the company solicitor or accountant. In larger companies, company secretary is a full-time job, and the tendency nowadays is for the position to be filled by a person with legal training rather than one with a financial background as was the case in the past. The company auditor may not be the company secretary. In the case of a public company the 1985 Act imposes on directors the duty to appoint a person with the requisite knowledge and experience. The intention of the legislation is that a company secretary should always be a professionally qualified person, although it does provide for some exceptions.

The company secretary may also be given responsibility for other functional matters such as insurance and pensions.

The company secretary often acts as secretary of subsidiary companies and board subcommittees. The effect of this should be to minimise errors or omissions which can occur through a lack of intercompany communication, and to ensure the board's proper overall control of statutory and legal matters.

Functions of the board

It has been established that the board is responsible for the conduct of the business. It cannot avoid that responsibility. Even if tasks are delegated or assigned, the ultimate responsibility remains with the controlling board (or group board if there are subsidiary companies).

The principal functions of the board can be summarised as follows:

— setting the objectives of the company
— determining the strategy by which those objectives will be achieved
— approving the plans for implementing the strategy, including budgets, forecasts and cash flows
— monitoring progress against the plans, with particular emphasis on margins, overhead expenses and cash flows

- defining those matters reserved for decision or approval by the board
- determining policies on issues relating to the company's trading activities and its internal use of resources
- approval of the year's results and the directors' report (the chairman's statement may not be the subject of board approval, but it is always available to the directors for comment prior to issue)
- relationship with shareholders
- mergers and acquisitions
- appointing directors
- approving the tasks and responsibilities assigned to directors
- company financing
- application of the company seal (for which a register must be kept).

The corporate business plan is of crucial importance to the discharge of the board's responsibilities. It brings together many interrelated matters in a single document (or perhaps two documents). It contains outline plans for, say, three or five years, and detailed plans for the coming financial year. The board needs to set aside plenty of time for discussion and adoption of the plan. Indeed, it is often decided that a separate meeting should be held to deal with this one issue.

Matters reserved to the board
The extent to which the board becomes involved in decision making depends on the complexity of the operation, the skills and experience of directors and managers and the areas in which the company is seen to be vulnerable. Having said that, most boards wish to be involved in the following:
- senior executive appointments
  Because of the various ways which exist of 'packaging' executive appointments, the board may well wish to approve the particular terms and conditions.
- investment programmes
  Approval in principle may have been given in the annual plan, but the board is normally asked to approve 'material' expenditure (as defined by the board).
- performance appraisal of directors and certain key managers
- manpower development and succession plans
  The company's success requires the proper development of personnel resources and the early identification of potential succession weaknesses.
- determining key decision points in any long-term programme, and reviewing the situation before committing further resources
- new business activities, and disengagement from existing businesses
- communications policies
- design policies
- computer policies
- public relations
- legal actions
  Actions which appear trivial can have quite disproportionate consequences.
- insurance covers
  The consequences of omitting to cover certain risks can be very damaging, particularly when trading internationally. The subject should be brought to the board periodically, perhaps every two or three years, possibly after independent professional review.
- management structure

- product pricing policies (these may be included in the business plan)

The revenue stream is a very significant factor in trading success. It is also the most difficult to predict with any accuracy.

The appointment of directors

The law relating to the role of directors and officers is contained in the Companies Act 1985. Overriding consideration of the legislation in relation to limited liability companies (that is, those companies registered under the act whereby the liability of the shareholders is limited) is the protection of company creditors. Directors' responsibilities towards employees are also covered.

The Companies Act provides that:

- a private company must have at least one director and a public company not less than two
- every company must have a secretary (and a sole director may not act in both capacities)
- even if there is subsequently found to be a defect in his appointment, acts of a director prior thereto are deemed valid
- every director before being appointed must sign a consent form for filing with the Registrar
- a director cannot be 'voted off' the board by his colleagues
- a director may be removed from office by an ordinary resolution (notwithstanding any agreement or provision in the Articles to the contrary) provided that special notice is given to the shareholders
- except in the case of a private company a director may not serve after reaching age 70 unless his appointment, of which notice has been given, is approved in general meeting
- except with the provision of the Court, an undischarged bankrupt may not act as a director
- except with permission of the Court, a person convicted of fraud may not act as a director or officer of any company for a period up to five years
- a director may not be paid by the company 'free of income tax'. Any sums so paid shall be deemed to be such gross sum as, after deduction of income tax, amounts to the payment actually made
- a register must be kept showing specified details of each director and officer of the company
- any person shall be liable as a director if he assumes the role of director, being a person 'in accordance with whose directions or instructions the directors are accustomed to act'.

Meetings

Effective meetings need thorough preparation and organisation. They should be held because there is value in a particular group of people coming together to exchange views and consider a problem. The end result should be positive — meetings should not be a way of avoiding decisions and actions.

The agenda should be issued five to seven days before the meeting in order to give all those participating enough time to prepare themselves. Supporting papers should be issued with the agenda to ensure that the meeting is able to concentrate on clarifying the facts and discussing the issues, rather than supplying information. This also avoids verbal reporting which can be vague and confusing.

Board meetings

The frequency ot board meetings will be dictated by the nature and organisation of the company. In some cases quarterly meetings are thought to be sufficient but, unless the board is essentially that of a holding company and the principal activities within the group are conducted by competent subsidiary boards meeting more frequently, quarterly meetings are unlikely to prove adequate.

In fairly small companies, meetings should take place monthly — this may in practice reduce to ten or so times a year. There are almost always enough issues of sufficient importance arising in a four-week period to warrant a board meeting. This is the proper way for a board to discharge its responsibilities. It may be necessary for the board to meet more frequently than monthly if there are special problems or difficulties to be resolved. It is highly desirable to fix the dates of board meetings for up to 12 months ahead. This helps busy executives and non-executive directors to plan their work better and to make a more worthwhile contribution to the meetings. Trying to bring together five or six busy people at short notice is a difficult exercise. Once a date has been fixed well in advance, only in extreme circumstances should it be changed. The fact that one director cannot be present should not affect the timing, and when it is clear the board intends to organise itself in this way, directors will build their own programmes around the scheduled dates.

Certain documents should be issued to the board several days before the meeting:

— management accounts
— operating reports by the managing director and preferably also by the key directors
— reports and recommendations on specific matters requiring decision.

This permits routine work to be disposed of efficiently, leaving the major part of the meeting for important issues, future developments and so on.

Of the ten to twelve meetings in the year, some should be principally concerned with key matters such as annual accounts, corporate plans, research and development, the product competition, the budget for the ensuing year or manpower. In this way the year's board work can be outlined right at the beginning. With good paper work and effective presentation it is possible to cover a great deal of ground.

Minutes should, of course, be issued after each meeting. Speed in producing the minutes helps to communicate the 'atmosphere' of the discussions. Minutes can be quite formal and brief — effectively just recording the decisions. Or they can be quite full. In small companies full minutes tend to be most useful. They should not normally name the individuals in an exchange of views, although on occasion this may be necessary. It requires considerable skill correctly to summarise difficult and lengthy discussions. Minutes should be as brief as is necessary properly to record the principal conclusion and the reasoning leading to it. A summary of the discussion of each item and its conclusion should be made by the chairman before the meeting proceeds; this ensures the meeting does agree at the time on a fair summing up and helps greatly with the task of minute writing. In any event, the minutes should not be issued until the chairman has approved them.

Subcommittees of the board

The procedures used by subcommittees are basically the same as those of the entire board meeting. Minutes may be issued, perhaps to the board as a whole, certainly to the chairman. Reports will be made to the main board from time to time if the minutes are not circulated.

Management meetings
There is almost invariably a need for weekly meetings of key managers, preferably on the same day each week. Good internal communication and exchanges of information provide the whole executive with a common base of knowledge. These meetings should not usually take a long time. Brief minutes should be issued immediately with action points and responsibility identified. Progress review each week is then relatively easy.

Other meetings
Many other meetings between certain directors or executives are convened to deal with specific problems. It is an obvious but important point to make that all concerned should be quite clear about the purpose of any meeting. Whoever calls the meeting and decides on its composition should issue a concise note as to its terms of reference and its purpose. If such a note is not issued, the chairman should start the meeting by defining its purpose and obtaining agreement on this from his colleagues. Preparing for a meeting in these ways avoids wasting time and makes for more valuable discussion. Good concise briefing is always very important.

Many business problems can be resolved by telephone discussion – perhaps in a conference hook-up – but on other occasions face-to-face exchanges are more satisfactory. In either case, brief meeting notes should always be issued.

Although consensus should always be sought, there are occasions when the chairman has to acknowledge the differing opinions of the meeting and make his own decision.

Reports to the board

Regular reports
The board must establish the nature, form and frequency of the reports and information which it needs. This should be done very early in its life even if it is not possible initially to supply all the information needed. With an established format, amended as the company develops, management can plan effectively.

Information required by management in quite small companies may be the same as that required by the board, but as business activities develop, management at lower levels needs more detail. The board should not be burdened with too much detail, but must be provided with enough information to understand what is happening and the extent of any deviation from plan.

In terms of routine financial reporting, the board will at least need to know:

- profit and loss (in period and cumulatively) with material variations from budget/plan
- order intake analysis and backlog
- sales revenue analysis
- gross margins
- cash flows (in period and cumulatively)
- cash forecasts (at least quarterly)
- balance sheet

- key ratios
  debtor and creditor positions and their duration.

This is covered in more detail in Chapter 7. There should be a report from the principal manager and preferably more detailed reports from the executive directors, with the managing director homing in on key issues and action programmes. Visual aids provide reinforcement of the written word.

Special reports

If meetings are structured as indicated above, special reports are necessary on the specific subject matters the board is scheduled to discuss. The aim of all such reports should be to direct attention to the key issues to be resolved and the management's recommended action to deal with them. Reports may be requested by the board itself, but it is more likely and preferable that the initiative comes from management.

It may be useful to establish a general format for all internal reports; this can make rapid assimilation easier and help to ensure that reports contain all the necessary information. The format could include:

- the subject matter of the report
- the object of the report
- a statement of the key background issues
- consideration of the factors relevant to the problem
- consideration of the alternative solutions, and a statement of the one preferred
- an outline of the plan to effect that solution with key dates
- financial implications.

When the report is completed, it should be checked to ensure that the solution matches the stated object.

Management performance

The key to running a successful business is the creation of an effective management team. This is a prime responsibility of the board. The board's appointment of managing director is crucial, and it will also take an interest in the appointment of principal subordinate managers.

New recruits to the board must be approved by all its members. Business in the boardroom is conducted in a formal way, but it is rare for directors to resort to counting votes. This means that close working relationships are essential between board members; they must have absolute confidence in each other's integrity in dealing with often very sensitive matters. If this trust and confidence are lacking, a board rapidly ceases to act effectively.

There are two sayings which every manager should bear in mind: 'There are no bad soldiers — only bad officers' and 'You cannot delegate — only assign responsibilities'. A manager can never cease to be responsible for a job which he may choose to give to someone else to perform.

In other words, the quality of management is extremely important and, as such, needs to be measured. It is surprising how many managers are reluctant to assess and discuss performance with each subordinate. Performance should be assessed according to agreed criteria and then discussed. Failure to do this is irresponsible and quite unfair to the subordinate himself. This matter is discussed in greater depth in Chapter 8.

Subsidiary companies

Subsidiary companies exist for many reasons. They may result from acquisitions which it makes commercial sense to continue to operate as separate entities. They may be created to provide for minority shareholders in a particular area of activity. They are frequently used in multi-product companies where it is commercially sensible to identify a particular product or marketing activity. They have disadvantages such as the administrative burden of having to produce consolidated accounts and a more complicated taxation situation. Generally, the same commercial purposes can be achieved without the need to form separate subsidiary companies. It is perfectly feasible to manage a group of related activities without giving each its own corporate structure.

In structuring a subsidiary board (or a divisional board without legal entity) the following elements should be considered for inclusion:

— managers of the particular activity
— group management, eg the group marketing director and group finance director (possibly providing its chairman)
— representation from activities in the group with whom there is a common business interest.

The secretarial aspect of the subsidiary should be keyed into the group secretarial office to ensure that statutory requirements are complied with. This may best be done by the group secretary also acting for the subsidiary.

Whereas a group of companies will normally be considered as a single entity from a financial point of view, the fact is that each company is a separate legal entity and, in the absence of parent company guarantees, stands on its own so far as creditors are concerned. Therefore, when trading or making contracts with a subsidiary company, care needs to be taken by third parties to guard against the risk of the company being allowed to become insolvent. This is perhaps of greatest importance in the case of foreign subsidiary companies: the parent company, for one reason or another, may not wish to stand fully behind its own child. It is more difficult to enforce agreements through the legal process of another country. The true ownership of a company may even be elsewhere — for example in the Cayman Islands — which makes the pursuit of rights even more difficult. Sometimes a company will sell a business to a third party, leaving the legal entity as no more than a shell. There are many traps for the unwary lurking behind limited liability, whether in the UK or elsewhere.

The directors of a subsidiary company need to consider the situation which frequently arises of the parent company moving all surplus funds into the holding company, with the subsidiary showing on the balance sheet not cash but a loan to the parent. Under certain circumstances, that loan may be risky or irrecoverable.

International operations

Although the principles of managing overseas operations are similar to those employed at home, the facts of geography, language, law and culture present some significant differences which have to be taken into account.

Whereas some years ago it would be the norm for overseas activities to be managed by an executive drawn from the UK, this is now less likely to be the case: standards of management in Europe and the USA are at least as good as in the UK, and the advantages of having an indigenous manager are considerable. This trend is likely to continue with UK nationals being employed only in positions where skills or knowledge cannot be obtained locally. Similarly, for the time being, it is likely that Japanese operations in the UK will be managed by nationals of that country because of the evident absence of comparable manufacturing skills here: in that case the advantages to the UK are evident.

It is very important for the parent company to understand the many differences that exist between business in the UK and most other countries. The UK manager abroad must have some experience of practical business situations in the country to which he is sent before he can communicate effectively.

Working knowledge of at least one European language is a distinct, but regrettably quite rare, asset among UK managers. While knowledge of English among foreign executives can almost be taken for granted nowadays, a UK manager able to communicate in the local language has a great advantage.

Engaging in overseas business requires extensive travel. There is no other way to acquire the feel and understanding essential to good management and good business. Expect to encounter professional standards.

Quite small companies find themselves seeking a significant part of their profit outside the UK. Overseas operations tend to involve foreign equity participation. In the case of the US it is practically impossible to run a successful business without management participation leading to capital gain. On the other hand, by such methods experienced and high calibre managers can be attracted to quite small and risky situations. When starting business it will be essential to work with good local advisers — considerably more expensive than in the UK — and venture capitalists. The US market in particular presents problems of scale which are very daunting; great caution and careful study are advised before embarking on business there.

Overseas business requires more time and effort and usually involves a participative form of management.

Joint interests

Although there have been very satisfactory and successful ventures owned on a 50/50 basis, it is widely accepted that control is essential. That involves, as a minimum, more than 50 per cent of voting capital, and a higher proportion is needed if extraordinary or special corporate business is to be carried with certainty.

There are many differing circumstances by which control can be achieved, from a casting vote by the chairman to a structure in which an apparently equal ownership can be presented as a controlled operation by both parties, or in which profits are divided by some formula to the greater benefit of one of the parties.

An operation in a foreign country may best be started as a controlled operation, reducing that control over a period of time as funding required to continue development becomes beyond the resources of the UK parent.

Once in a minority position, it is not very significant whether the holding is 49, 40 or 30 per cent. There is certainly a case for having at least a blocking vote by holding a proportion of the voting stock which will prevent material alterations in the structure of the business against the wishes of the minority interest.

It is important to recognise the special value which lies with control. The sale of a minority interest almost always suffers a substantial discount for that reason, whereas the sale of a marginal percentage which has the effect of giving control to the purchaser carries a substantial premium.

A holding of 20 per cent or more in a minority situation is usually satisfactory. Anything less than 10 per cent is fairly unimportant unless, of course, the shareholdings are widely distributed in packets of more or less equal size. It is wise to ensure that the interests of the parties are properly regulated through a shareholders' agreement, in addition to the Articles of Association. In private companies it is normal to prevent the free marketing of shares by requiring a vendor first to offer his shares to all the other members before being able to sell to a third party — this provides the opportunity to protect the balance of the shareholdings, which will have been carefully constructed.

Reporting to shareholders

The Companies Act 1981 made very significant changes in the format of the accounts, the contents of notes to the accounts and the directors' report to the shareholders. These changes are now embodied in the 1985 Act.

Exemptions

A company may qualify to be treated as a small or medium-sized company if it satisfies the criteria set out below. It is then entitled to certain accounting exemptions. As a result of the exemptions, the company may file modified accounts with the Registrar of Companies, but unmodified accounts must still be presented to the shareholders.

A company is not eligible for the accounting exemptions if it is or was at any time during the accounting reference period:

- a public company
- a banking, insurance or shipping company
- a member of a group which, inter alia, contains a company ineligible under (a) or (b) above.

Qualifying conditions for exemption

To qualify for exemption as a small or medium-sized company in respect of a particular financial year, it must, for that year and the immediately preceding financial year, satisfy at least two of the following qualifying conditions:

		Small	Medium-sized
(i)	Turnover not exceeding	£1.4 million	£5.75 million
(ii)	Balance sheet totals not exceeding	£700,000	£2.8 million
(iii)	Average number of employees (on a weekly basis) not exceeding	50	250

Small company exemptions

The following modifications are permitted in the accounts delivered to the Registrar:

- Balance sheet — confined to items specifically identified in the prescribed format (of the 1985 Act)
- Profit and loss account — not required
- Notes to the accounts — restricted to:
    (i) accounting policies

   (ii) share capital
  (iii) substantial investments in other companies
  (iv) aggregate creditors falling due after more than five years
   (v) secured creditors
  (vi) ultimate holding company
 (vii) loans to directors and officers
(viii) *aggregate of debtors due after more than one year
  (ix) *if formula 2 (as defined in the Act) is adopted, aggregate of creditors due within one year and after one year.

* may be shown in the balance sheet

— directors' report — not required
— auditors' report — a special report.

Medium-sized company exemptions

The only modifications permitted are:

— several specific items in the profit and loss format may be combined to give one heading 'gross profit or loss' (the items referred to differ according to which of the four accounting formats has been adopted)
— disclosure and analysis of turnover is not required.

True and fair view

The overriding principle applying to the preparation of accounts is that they should present 'a true and fair view of the financial position and profit or loss'. Modified accounts for small and medium-sized companies described above are not intended to give a true and fair view and, in the case of small companies in particular, may well not do so. Although they are based on shareholders' accounts which must comply with statements of standard accounting practice (SSAPs), they need not themselves include disclosures or statements required by SSAPs.

Balance sheet

The balance sheet delivered to the Registrar must be signed by two directors of the company (or by the sole director) with a statement immediately above the signature(s) to the effect that the directors have relied on the exemptions and that the company is entitled to the exemptions (either as a small or medium-sized company as the case may be).

Without going into detail, the special auditor's report must include a statement to the effect that the exemption requirements are satisfied.

The directors' report

Typically, the directors' report to the shareholders will include:

— results for the period, recommended dividend and proposed transfer to reserves
— review of the business (including a definition of the company's principal activity and any significant changes therein during the year)
— changes in share capital
— market values of land and buildings: substantial differences between book and market value

- significant changes in fixed assets
- research and development expenditure: policy and purpose
- future developments
- significant events since the year end
- directors and their interests, including changes during the year
- policy applied to disabled persons (companies with fewer than 250 employees exempt)
- a statement as to how the company has pursued arrangements for informing, consulting and involving employees in the business (companies with fewer than 250 employees exempt)
- political and charitable contributions
- appointment of auditors
- particulars of the company's own shares purchased during the year.

The report must be signed by a director or on behalf of the board by the company secretary.

The auditors are required to check the directors' report for consistency with the accounts and to report any inconsistencies.

Publication of accounts

There are certain restrictions on the publication of accounts, particularly that when submitted to shareholders or filed with the Registrar they must have attached the relevant audit report.

The chairman's statement

There are no legal requirements relating to the chairman's statement. There need not be one. He may or may not replace it with a verbal statement at the annual general meeting.

If the chairman does issue a statement, it deals with issues not covered in the directors' report except, perhaps, to place special emphasis on particular aspects of that report.

The chairman normally seeks comment from some or all of the directors when drafting the statement, but he is under no obligation to do so. The statement is personal to him. It is usual for the auditors to see the statement ahead of issue, and obviously they would draw his attention to matters at variance with the accounts.

There is no doubt that shareholders and others pay a great deal of attention to the contents of the chairman's statement.

Interim statements

Companies quoted on the Stock Exchange or traded on the Unlisted Securities Market must conform with regulations issued by the Stock Exchange. The main purpose of the regulations is to ensure that adequate information about companies is available to all intending to deal in their securities, and that all have access to that information at the same time. For that reason care must be exercised in the granting of press or stockbroker interviews.

Conclusion

This chapter has ranged over a broad spectrum of important issues to show that the competence of the board and management are at the root of business effectiveness. One of the chief causes of failure among small businesses is a board which is weak, indecisive or lacking in balance.

Chapter 3

The Meaning of Figures

Finance and financial knowledge do not make a business, which is all about servicing customers. But finance is one of the two main pillars around which a business is constructed — the other being people.

Financial control is essential to the running of a sound business enterprise. Many managers, especially in small companies, have only a poor understanding of financial matters. This is surely one of the factors causing the long-term deterioration in the UK international performance.

While this book cannot consider in any depth the complex subject of finance, this chapter attempts to establish those aspects which must be understood by managers and, in particular, the managing director.

The international language of business is figures. The competent manager must have a fundamental understanding of figures; financial matters cannot be left to the accountant alone.

External professional advice may be necessary from time to time but in the daily management of the business, managing director and senior managers need to have had some financial training. The accountant must make his contribution by presenting financial information as accurately and as simply as possible to busy managers who carry responsibility for running the business; he cannot assume an understanding of accounting concepts or of accountants' jargon.

The directors need to know their responsibilities in terms of company law and other relevant commercial law. The company secretary is expected to provide advice in this field but this is not sufficient. The managing director should arrange, as part of the manpower development programme, to provide directors with some knowledge of law and finance as they affect the business.

The balance sheet

The balance sheet shows the assets, liabilities and shareholders' funds employed in the business. It is effectively a snapshot of the position at a particular point in time. The day before, or the day after, the position is almost certain to be different — possibly materially so.

The balance sheet does not purport to represent the value of the business. It merely states the balances as shown in the books of the company. The policies which have brought about those balances are disclosed in the notes to the accounts.

Assets
Assets can be grouped broadly under three headings:

   — *Fixed assets:* such as premises, factory and office equipment and motor vehicles. They are those assets by the use of which the business is conducted.

It is not appropriate to revalue fixed assets on a regular basis. The accounting concept is to write down the book cost of an asset over its estimated useful life, the reductions being designated as depreciation or amortisation, depending on the nature of the asset. The balance sheet description will then be 'at cost, less depreciation'.

Infrequently, revaluation may be desirable, particularly in the case of freehold and leasehold premises. In such cases, the notes and balance sheet will indicate that fact.

— *Current assets:* which arise in the course of trading activity. For example, stocks, debtors and that element of payments made in advance and therefore carried forward to a future period (prepayments).

Unlike fixed assets, current assets are valued at their estimated realisable value at the balance sheet date, subject to one overriding prudent accounting concept, namely, that current assets are not valued in excess of cost. The general principle is known as 'cost or market value, whichever is the lesser'. Thus, unrealised profits on current assets are not anticipated.

— *Intangible assets:* which do not conveniently fall into either of the categories described, such as patent rights, trade marks, goodwill and so on.

By their nature, these are difficult to value, but can be very valuable. They are carried at cost, and written down over defined periods of time. The item 'goodwill' most frequently arises through the process of company acquisition, where the price paid is in excess of the net asset cost as shown in the books. An acquired company, for tax or trading reasons, often continues its separate existence. The price paid in excess of the net asset cost is usually described in the balance sheet of the acquiring company as 'excess cost of acquisition' (see consolidation below) and best accounting practice is to write it off immediately or as soon as possible over a period of time.

Funding (liabilities and shareholders)

The balance sheet sets out to show how the funding of the assets has taken place. There are three broad categories of funding sources:

— *Shareholders:* the amounts subscribed by way of capital, and other accumulated reserves which are attributed to ownership of the company. Accumulated retained revenue surpluses are shown under this heading, as being attributable to the ordinary shareholders. So also are other capital and revenue reserves. Appendix A describes in greater detail the interests of shareholders.

— *Loans:* medium- and long-term loans are shown and described in detail in notes to the accounts. For this purpose, amounts falling due for payment more than 12 months after the date of the balance sheet will be shown in this grouping. Many loans are secured either on specific assets or by a general charge over all the assets; this fact will be disclosed.

Loans can be raised outside the UK and be designated and repayable in a foreign currency. These loans carry the risk of unfavourable changes in exchange rates.

— *Current liabilities:* arising, like current assets, in the course of trading.

Trade creditors and provisions for expenses which have been incurred but not paid at balance sheet date are typical. Bank overdraft finance, which should essentially be short-term, will also be shown as a current liability.

Because accounts are kept on the double-entry principle, the totals of assets and liabilities will, of course, agree.

In addition to the above, there are often potential or contingent liabilities which could be material. For example, at the point when the balance sheet is drawn there may be a dispute or legal action pending or in process. There may also be un-certainty as to whether or not a particular liability will arise, and how much it will be. In such cases, a reference to the item is given in the notes with, possibly, an indication of likely liability.

There are often other material items which do not appear in the balance sheet (off balance sheet) but are covered in the notes. For example:

— guarantees which have been given by the company to a third party, but which have not crystallised.
— liabilities arising under leases. A lease entered into carries with it future obligations for the payment of rent and repairs. There may or may not be the unfettered right to assign the lease to some other person.
— liabilities arising from equipment leasing transactions. Until recently, it was usual to omit the asset and liability from the balance sheet, and to rely on its disclosure by way of note. The more common practice now is to disclose the transaction on the face of the balance sheet.

It is important to understand what the balance sheet reveals and what it does not. Equally essential is a careful reading of the notes attached to the balance sheet, because they will describe the accounting policies which have been adopted in its preparation.

It is now a requirement that a balance sheet cannot be finalised without regard to events which it is anticipated may take place after the date of the balance sheet and which would have an effect on it. If these post-balance sheet events are material, it is necessary either to adjust the balance sheet or to deal with them in the attached notes. This remains the position until the accounts are finally signed off by the directors and the auditors.

Because business situations vary so much it is not possible to standardise every-thing to do with accounting treatment. However, considerable progress has been made in recent years towards standardisation through the issue by the principal accounting institutions of Standards of Accounting Practice applicable to UK companies. The overriding principle in the drawing of accounts is the concept of 'true and fair view'. This should at all times be the key to the disclosure of items likely to influence the reader. It is for the directors, and no one else, to present the accounts of the company and to take full responsibility for them. It is for the auditors to consider the accounts presented to them and to report on them. In practice, of course, there will be discussion between the directors and the auditors as accounts are prepared in order to limit areas of potential conflict; many items are essentially matters of judgement, and the directors need to understand the full implications of what is stated in the company's accounts.

Accounting policies

The accounting policies adopted by the company in determining the amounts to be included in respect of items shown in the balance sheet and in determining the profit or loss of the company shall be stated (including such policies with respect to the depreciation and diminution in value of assets). Companies Act 1985 Schedule 4.

The accounting principles to be adopted are also set out in Schedule 4 (Part II) to the 1985 Act.

In 1971 the Accounting Standards Committee defined the 'fundamental accounting concepts' as being the basic assumptions which underlie the periodic financial accounts of business enterprises.

The following are the four fundamental concepts:

— *The 'going concern' concept:* this means that the profit and loss account and balance sheet assume no intention or necessity to liquidate or curtail significantly the scale of the business operation.
— *the 'accruals' concept:* revenue and costs are recognised as they are earned or incurred (not when received or paid in cash); matched with one another (so far as can be established or reasonably assumed); dealt with in the profit and loss account of the period to which they relate.
— *the 'consistency' concept:* that there is consistency of accounting treatment of like items within each accounting period and from one period to another.
— *the 'prudence' concept:* revenue and profits are not anticipated, but recognised only when realised in the form of cash or of other assets, the ultimate cash realisation of which can be assessed with reasonable certainty. Provision is made for all known liabilities, whether the amount of these is known with certainty or is a best estimate in the light of the information available.

If accounts are prepared on the basis of assumptions which differ in material respects from any of the accepted concepts, the facts must be explained. In the absence of any such explanation, it will be assumed that the four fundamental concepts have been observed.

The application of accounting standards and policies is governed by the question of 'materiality', which was first given formal recognition in the Companies Act 1948. It is neither possible nor desirable to seek a close definition of materiality. It can be stated that, in an accounting sense, a matter is material if its non-disclosure, misstatement or omission would be likely to distort the view given in the context of a particular situation — it is also a psychological concept. A ship stuck in the Arabian Gulf will be viewed very differently from one sailing freely in pursuit of its trade, although in every other respect the two ships may be similar and have the same book value. Knowledge of certain information can clearly change the perception of values.

Consolidation

Consolidating the accounts of a group of companies is required by law, in the case of companies which control (usually by owning more than 50 per cent of the voting shares) one or more other companies. Consolidated accounts set out to show, in one statement, the position of the group as if it were trading as a single entity. An 'excess cost of acquisition' (goodwill) as referred to above is almost always shown in these accounts. Consolidating the accounts of a large number of companies, perhaps in foreign currencies which have to be translated into the currency of the holding company, is a complex exercise.

It must be understood that such a presentation does not affect the separate legal identity of each subsidiary company and the holding company. UK law requires the preparation of a separate set of accounts for each of these.

Because this accounting process has to take place so soon after one company acquires control of another, quite small businesses find themselves preparing consolidated accounts.

In many cases subsidiary companies are owned 100 per cent. If, however, they are not, but there is nevertheless effective control, the process of consolidation shows that part of the group which it does not own as a separate item in the consolidated balance sheet. It is described as 'minority interests' and is shown with the liabilities, because it purports to represent third party claims on the assets of the group.

The following illustrates the principle of the item 'excess cost of investment'.

Assume a company has a balance sheet as follows:

	£
Assets	50,000
Liabilities	30,000
Net worth	20,000
(attributable to shareholders)	

If the company is purchased by another at a price of £30,000, then when the assets and liabilities of the acquired company are consolidated into those of the purchasing company, the excess cost of acquisition will appear as £10,000:

	£
Cost of investment	30,000
Underlying net assets	20,000
Excess cost of acquisition	10,000

If on the same data the purchasing company bought only 70 per cent of the company for a price of £21,000 the two basic differences in presentation in the consolidated balance sheet would be:

Excess cost of acquisition	£7,000
(£21,000 less 70 per cent of £20,000 net worth)	

and on the liability side there would be:

Interests of minority shareholders	£6,000
(representing 30 per cent of £20,000 net worth)	

Associated companies

Holdings of less than 50 per cent but greater than 20 per cent are accorded the special status of an 'associated company'. They cannot be fully consolidated into the accounts of the group because the vital ingredient of control is absent. However, the ownership of 20 per cent or more of the voting shares is significant and makes it 'a related company'. Essentially, the characteristics are that the investment is intended to be held on a long-term basis for the purpose of securing commercial benefit to the investor by the exercise of control or significant influence, that is by participating in the policy decisions affecting that investment.

Such interests will be accounted for in the consolidated accounts by the 'equity method'. This method requires that the investment is recorded in the books at cost, and the balance sheet is adjusted each year by the amount of the investor's share in the profits (or losses) of the associated company subsequent to acquisition. The incremental amount thus shown is likewise reflected in the profit and loss account.

Adjustments may also be required in respect of reserve movements and the excess cost of the acquisition over the appropriate share of net assets of the associated company. It should be noted that no such adjustments should be made in the legal accounts of the investing company.

Other investments

If the ownership is less than 20 per cent the investment is shown simply as an asset held by the company. No attempt is made to incorporate it into the statements of the owning company: it is treated as a 'fixed' or 'current' asset depending on the purposes for which it is held. Income arising from these investments in the form of dividends will be identified as such in the income statement. The parent company's investments may therefore be summarised thus:

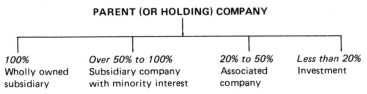

Figure 3.1. *Investment categories*

Comments on the balance sheet

Total assets	— The gross amount of all the assets shown in the balance sheet: effectively the totals at the foot of the balance sheet.
Net assets	— Total assets less liabilities. These may be alternatively referred to as 'net worth' or 'shareholders' interests'.
Net tangible assets	— As for net assets, but deducting intangible assets appearing in the balance sheet. A common yardstick used by lenders.
Working capital	— Current assets less current liabilities. This is a very important indicator of liquidity. Working capital is fundamentally associated with cash flow (as discussed in Chapter 6).
Shareholders' funds	— Discloses separately the interests of ordinary, preference and deferred shares to the extent they are in issue. Subject to the prior repayment rights of any preference shares in the event of liquidation, the accumulated capital and revenue reserves will effectively be attributed to the ordinary shareholders (frequently referred to as the equity).
Gearing	— The relationship of borrowed monies to shareholders' funds. The prudent ratio of the one to the other is a matter of judgment in any particular business, but a general guideline in an established business might be the ratio 1:2. If the gearing is conservative the earning yield on shareholders'

funds is being adversely affected. If the gearing is high, the yield on shareholders' funds is enhanced, but the business is being run at a higher risk.

Fixed assets, because of their nature, should be financed by shareholders' funds or by medium- to long-term borrowings.

Working capital should be partly financed by bank overdraft or short-term borrowings: but some shareholders' funds may be applied to finance part of the working capital.

Net operating assets — Refers to those net assets actively employed in the business. The definition differs from net assets by the subtraction of cash balances or overdrafts, as the case may be. Its value is to determine the assets actually employed in running the business and how effectively they are being used by calculating their rate of turnover thus:

$$\frac{\text{Sales revenues per annum}}{\text{NOA}} = \text{Asset turn}$$

The greater the turnover rate, the lower the amount of capital required to run the business. This is, therefore, an important indicator of the effective management control of capital employed. More attention should be given by management to the effective use of capital.

The profit and loss account

Unlike the balance sheet drawn at a point in time, the profit and loss account is prepared to cover a period of time. The total profit for a period can be determined by comparing a balance sheet prepared at the beginning of a period with one prepared at the end. The difference in net worth is the amount of profit for the period.

The profit and loss account explains how that result comes about. It is obviously important to know this.

It can cover any period of time. By law a company must prepare accounts for presentation at an annual general meeting (although, contrary to general belief, they do not have to be approved or adopted by the shareholders). The directors must decide the date to which the accounts are made up (the accounting reference date). Once this has been fixed it is inadvisable, for comparison and tax purposes, to change the year end. It is usual, however, to change the accounting reference date of any subsidiary company acquired to coincide with that of the parent company; this assists the preparation of consolidated accounts and presents a more accurate picture of the group results.

The profit and loss account will be affected by the accounting policies and concepts adopted by the company, as set out in the notes to the accounts.

The overriding principle in preparing a profit and loss account is to match revenues with those costs incurred in earning them.

For ease of reading, the profit and loss account may be presented in as brief a form as will present a true and fair view, with more detailed data relegated to supporting schedules. (Presentation to shareholders must, of course, comply with the Companies Acts.)

A typical profit and loss account for a manufacturing and selling company could look like Figure 3.2

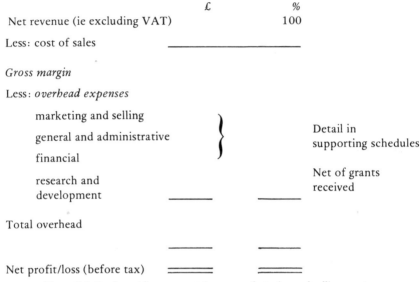

	£	%
Net revenue (ie excluding VAT)		100
Less: cost of sales	————————	
Gross margin		
Less: *overhead expenses*		
marketing and selling		
general and administrative		Detail in supporting schedules
financial		
research and development	———	———
		Net of grants received
Total overhead		
Net profit/loss (before tax)	══════	══════

Figure 3.2. *Profit and loss account for a manufacturing and selling company*

The nature of costs

Costs are broadly of three types:

Variable — those which respond more or less directly in relation to revenues, or can be adjusted in the short term

Fixed — those which are more or less fixed, and which therefore respond only slowly to movements in revenues

Semi-variable — those falling somewhere between those two categories.

It is extremely difficult to forecast revenues with any accuracy, because of the multiplicity of factors which can affect them, many of which are external and outside the control of the business itself. The ability to control and adjust costs rapidly is therefore critical to profitability, and more consideration will be given later to the methods aimed at achieving such control.

Variable costs

Materials forming part of the products which are to be sold should, in theory, respond rapidly to movements in sales revenues. The problem area is the extent to which stocks are necessary to ensure smooth production and distribution arrangements.

The retailer has a better chance than the manufacturer of reacting quickly. In the manufacturing process the lead time is likely to be longer. In either case effective stock control policies have to be operated, and management must be firm in seeing that the policies are being carried out.

When it is necessary to reduce costs quickly, it is often advertising which is cut because this has an immediate effect and can be done fairly easily. The great problem with advertising expenditure is that its effectiveness is very difficult to measure; part of it is almost bound to be unproductive, but nobody can be sure which part. So, while the importance of advertising to build or maintain turnover is recognised, when immediate cost reductions are necessary the short-term view often prevails, and advertising is reduced at the risk of creating future difficulties.

Employment legislation and the strength of trade unions have significantly affected the ability of business to react quickly to adverse trading conditions by shedding labour, and they have certainly added to the costs of doing so. In strongly unionised businesses it is wise now to regard employment as almost a semi-variable cost.

Fixed costs

Fixed costs relate, for example, to the provision of accommodation, factory space and other buildings. Clearly they do not respond at all in the short term to trends in the market-place, and can be adjusted only over a period of time. Many expenses are associated with space occupation, such as maintenance and repair, insurance, heating and ventilation.

The break-even point

The importance of the cost structure is to determine the business break-even point — the point at which revenues are just sufficient to cover the costs of the business. Beyond that point profits tend to go up at a faster rate since fixed costs remain the same and variable costs respond directly to revenues. This may be illustrated by Figure 3.3.

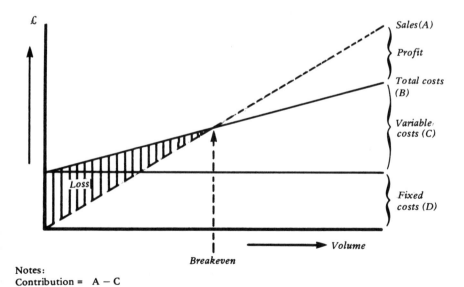

Notes:
Contribution = A − C
Net profit   = A − (C + D)

Figure 3.3. *The break-even point*

Gross margins and net margins

A manager will want to know the difference between gross and net sales revenues. He will want to know by product how much discounting is actually taking place in achieving orders. The determination of gross margin is critical. It is a key element in any business plan. But because most businesses handle more than one product, the overall result is dependent on the product mix actually being sold. The margin is unlikely to be the same on each individual product.

The planning of margins has to be related to each product. The gross profit arising from each product is known as 'the product contribution'. The sum of these contributions provides funds for the remaining overhead expenses. Adequate gross margins are essential if proper provision for future development is to be made.

The net margin is also very important. This is what remains of the gross margin after allowing for overhead costs and taxation. Subject to taxation, it is the source from which dividends are paid, and from which funds are taken to support future development.

The ratio of net profit to the capital in use in the business is a critical one for management to understand. An unsatisfactory ratio has serious implications for the long-term survival of a business and its ability to attract additional capital when needed. The relationship between overhead expenses and revenues is equally important.

It is often the case, in any business sector, that firms achieve similar ratios, and comparisons are worthwhile making. For example, in fast growing technology businesses the typical ratios might be:

Gross margins	50%+
Net margins (minimum)	15%
Selling expenses	20%
General and administrative costs	5% − 10%
Research and development costs	5% − 10%

Direct and indirect costs

Direct costs are those costs incurred which have a direct part in the manufacture or purchase of products which are subsequently sold by the business. Indirect costs are the many expenses necessary to the conduct of the business which do not play a direct part in the cost of the product.

Management must also be familiar with the following terms which show the progressive cost build-up of a product:

— *prime costs:* direct materials and direct labour only
— *factory costs:* including prime costs, plus costs incurred in the process of manufacture or assembly, from input to the factory to the point of output from the factory
— *total costs:* factory costs, plus all expenses necessary to the conduct of the business, incurred in the sales and general administrative functions.

Standard costs

The business of costing is not an exact science. Product costing has to be done on the basis of estimates. Fixed costs can seldom be allocated precisely; for example, factory throughput or loading has to be estimated. Effective manufacture may be assumed to be, say, 80 per cent. To the extent that volume turns out to be greater or less than this, there will be a favourable or unfavourable cost variance. Standard costs are constructed in this way and it is the only practical way of working. This means reviewing from time to time the assumptions on which the standard costs are based and adjusting to reality. It also means that the management needs to know regularly, in the periodic accounts, what variance has taken place. Standard cost variances can arise from a combination of causes, particularly from costs actually incurred and production volumes. These need to be separately identified.

The practical problems of costing are considerable. A complicated business operation with, for example, stocks held at different purchase prices, substantial work-in-progress at any point in time and so on, needs a specialist cost accountant, with a thorough knowledge of the factory process. Cost should not be the sole determinant of sales pricing policy, but it is certainly very important and must be properly understood.

Product contribution

It will be appreciated that, in the normal multi-product situation, the allocation of costs to products can at best be rather arbitrary, but it is nevertheless essential to be able to establish the gross profit and margin arising from each product. This is generally known as the product contribution. It is more reliable and of more value to assess the contribution from each product at the 'gross' stage. The sum of the contributions from several products can then be clearly established as the source from which all the remaining overhead costs can be serviced.

Thus the profit statement can be restated as shown in Figure 3.4.

	Turnover £	Gross margin %	Gross profit £	
Contributions				
Product 1				
Product 2				Ratio to
Product 3				turnover
etc	_____	_____	_____	%
	_____	_____	A	
Overhead costs				
Selling				
General				
Financial				
Research and development			_____	
Total overhead			B	
Net profit (A−B)			C	

Figure 3.4. Profit statement showing product contribution

Order intake

The order intake is vital, and there should be a supporting schedule (as indeed there will also be for product sales and contributions if the range of products is extensive) showing for the period something like that shown in Figure 3.5.

	O/S orders state at start	*Orders in period*	*Sales in period*	*O/S orders state at end*
Product 1				
Product 2				
Product 3				
etc				
Total				

Figure 3.5. *Order intake schedule by product*

This begins to give some valuable information about a key aspect of the business. It is more valuable when the cumulative position is also shown and comparisons with, for example, last year, budget and forecast are given. An additional section on the order state can show the 'cover' provided by order backlog, that is, the number of forward invoice periods held in backlog or the forward periods during which deliveries are likely to occur. This section might be headed: Next period: Next following period: Thereafter.

The same basic data can be used for different purposes. For instance, orders and sales need to be analysed by sales territory and/or salesman so that the manager can check progress and the reason for any departure from plan.

To provide important advance notice to management, the gross margin included in the period orders and in the backlog should be identified, product by product.

Source and application of funds

The balance sheet and profit and loss account provide the information needed for the preparation of a statement of the source and application of funds, the purpose of which is to show the sources of cash flow in the period and how these have been applied in the business, particularly how they have affected working capital.

It is necessary to start with the cash generated through trading and to adjust for those items of expense not giving rise to current cash movements (such as depreciation of assets which, although charged to the profit and loss account, does not involve any cash outgoing — this occurred when the asset was purchased).

Other sources of funding will arise from such items as:

— new capital raised
— assets sold
— borrowed monies.

The application of those funds is then identified by, for example, the purchase costs of fixed assets, and the movements which have taken place in the key areas comprising the working capital of the business, that is:

— stocks
— debtors
— creditors.

The important factor thus revealed is the movement in liquidity. Statements of this nature allow the board to review regularly the cash flows through the business, one of the acid tests of business control. Appendix 2 illustrates a pro forma layout of a funds control statement.

Ratios

From the data in the balance sheet and profit and loss account it is possible to calculate important financial ratios. These provide a vital indication of the health of the business, and must therefore be made available at an early date after each period.

Appendix 3 lists a number of key ratios from which management should select the keys to performance measurement and monitor regularly. Appendix 3 also gives an example of the use of ratios for comparative purposes; a study of this example reveals some significant trends.

Figure 3.6 is a summary of the points to be considered if, for example, an increase is required in net profits in relation to net operating assets (which may be considered more valuable as an efficiency measure than the more usual base of capital employed).

Improve trading results			Reduce net operating assets	
Increase sales	Reduce costs		Fixed	Working Capital
	Fixed	Variable		
1. Higher net prices and/or	1. More efficient use of facilities	1. Better procurement	1. Improve use or location of land and buildings	1. Reduce debtors
2. Greater volume through	2. Improve work effectiveness	2. More efficient use of labour and materials	2. Improve use of machines	2. Increase creditors
3. Better control	3. Apply information technology	3. Better product engineering	3. Modernise machines	3. More efficient use of stocks
4. Better marketing			4. Computer applications to production	4. Improve trading terms for cash flow
5. New products				

Figure 3.6. *Summary of relevant sources of net profit improvement in relation to NOA*

The key relationship between profit and asset use is thus established:

Net profit margin x NOA turnover rate = Profit return on net operating assets

The ratios are:

$$\frac{\text{Net profits}}{\text{Sales}} \quad x \quad \frac{\text{Sales}}{\text{NOA}}$$

Suppose these ratios are:

12%   x   4   =   48% on NOA

Quite small movements in either or both will have significant effect, eg:

13%   x   4.5   =   58.5% (or +21.9%).

Such improvements will be brought about only through detailed analysis of the elements entering into the calculation of each ratio.

Marginal costing

It is worth making a brief reference to the question of marginal costs. In a going concern, long-term viability depends on a proper recovery through pricing of all costs entering into the product for sale. But there are circumstances which justify a departure from this principle, pricing being fixed with only variable costs being taken into account. This practice of marginal pricing must be given careful consideration, because obviously it cannot be applied on a regular basis across all products. It may be useful when attempting to open up a new market or to establish an improved market position. It requires firm control from senior management and the risks must be assessed and monitored regularly.

Termination costs

It is useful on some occasions to determine the 'disaster cost', that is, the maximum total loss which could arise in the event that revenue volumes fail to materialise at the planned level and the business or activity must be terminated. Revenues are very difficult to predict at any time, and are always the most suspect part of any plan. This is especially true with new activities. Predictions usually turn out to have been optimistic, sometimes deliberately, sometimes not. The board is entitled to know, in addition to the planned results, and asset employment, what the financial bill will be if the operation is terminated. This must take into account both revenue and capital and include the many problems which arise only at termination, such as the realisable value of stocks and the difficulty in collecting debts. However remote the possibility, it is information which it is wise to have prepared.

Inflation

The UK has had to live with inflation for many years – sometimes very high inflation. It arises when governments issue bank notes in excess of the underlying growth in real national wealth. Businesses need to achieve financial results in 'real terms'. This means adjusting current results to account for inflation and make them properly comparable with a plan or with a previous period. Unadjusted results give a misleading, flattering impression.

At a time of inflation, the real cost of borrowing is reduced because a fixed capital sum is being repaid in depreciated currency. So with stocks. Stocks purchased at one price will, through changes in currency values, be sold at a higher price some time later, thus importing an inflationary bonus into the profit and loss account. The process will be repeated each time stocks are replaced.

On the other hand, because the replacement costs of assets will be rising, and amounts retained in the business through depreciation provisions are based on historic costs, there will be a shortfall in cash provision when the asset falls due for replacement. A mistake often made is to make an inadequate allowance in product costings for the higher asset replacement cost, so that product prices and margins are falsely calculated. Injections of new capital may then be necessary merely to keep the business afloat.

It is thus possible, and has happened in many companies in recent years, for dividends to be paid from non-existent profits (that is, partly or wholly — and illegally — out of capital), usually without the board being aware, or fully aware, of that fact. 'Current cost accounting' is a system for adjusting historic costs for the calculated inflationary element which has been adopted in a number of UK companies. It does not replace the historic system, but is used alongside it to show more faithfully the results of the business. However, after years of discussion, there is still not unanimity within the accounting profession about the best method of accounting for inflation.

Financing the business

We now consider some of the principles relevant to the funding of a business. It is not until a business plan has been drafted (see Chapter 4), leading to projected balance sheets, profit and loss accounts and cash flows, that the financial implications can be properly assessed. It is not normally satisfactory to rely on a one-year view: some reasoned forecast is needed for at least the two following years. A reasonable contingency plan must also be provided, because however carefully revenue estimates are prepared, their accuracy cannot be guaranteed.

The balancing of the funding requirement between the sources available is always difficult. Professional advice must be taken. If shareholders provide all the funds, borrowing risks are reduced but the earning of satisfactory returns is more difficult. If a high proportion is borrowed, the repayment and interest risks are considerably increased, but so are the rewards for success. The consequences of heavy borrowing when there is a rapid change in circumstances can be illustrated by the UK property collapse in 1974, which triggered the crisis in the secondary banking system. It is traditional for property developers to resort to significant bank borrowings in the course of developments: if the business is able to follow its planned programme, this results in satisfactory lettings, refinancing of the project on a long-term basis, and the emergence of a substantial gain on revaluation of the property. But if the market falters, lettings of speculative properties are not achieved, interest rates rise, and then almost immediately the developer runs into serious problems if the company's resources are inadequate.

Borrowing is all about confidence. As long as it is believed that a company can meet its obligations as they fall due, everything proceeds smoothly. But once rumours start to circulate that this is not the case — whether fact or not — trading immediately becomes difficult. Creditors become reluctant to extend their credit facilities and begin to press for earlier payment. They may refuse to grant further credit – cash with order only. Such steps immediately throw out of gear the established balance within the company for the financing of working capital. Conditions such as these require immediate and firm management action if a real crisis is to be avoided.

Management should have regard to the following borrowing principles:

- *Do not borrow short and invest long.* It is unsound to finance fixed assets by, say, short-term borrowings. In its overdraft agreement the bank will have the right to call its overdraft 'on demand'. As fixed assets cannot be realised at short notice nor probably at their book cost, the business will be at risk if circumstances turn out unfavourably.
- *Match currency borrowings with currency assets.* The risks attached to currency loans have already been considered. Running a business carries enough risks without incurring those which are unnecessary. It is correct to borrow, say, Deutschmarks for the purpose of investing in a business in West Germany. But to borrow Deutschmarks for the purposes of remitting them to the UK in sterling and investing in a sterling asset immediately opens up the risk of a potential liability of unknown quantity. It can be reduced by 'hedging' in forward Deutschmarks, but at a price. It is a practice to be avoided.

    In the same way, an insurer collecting premiums in, say, US dollars, with an obligation to settle future claims in US dollars, has to be very prudent about their investment because claims can arise over extended future periods at an unknown exchange rate.
- *Maintain a prudent ratio of borrowings to shareholders' funds.* As a general guide, for established businesses a ratio of 1:2 is probably advisable. The reason for this is that the cost of interest on the borrowings is a fixed charge, regardless of trading fortunes. Low sales revenues, for example, quickly affect the net profit position (because of the fixed and semi-variable costs).

    It is usual in loan agreements to establish the ratio of borrowings to net worth which may not be breached without giving the lender powerful rights against the company. In the case of overdraft facilities, reporting to the bank the trading and current asset data will be a regular requirement.

    Each case is different, and it would be wrong to say *never* depart from these principles. But any departure must be most carefully considered and the situation thereafter closely monitored.

Sources of finance

There is a wide variety of funding sources available to support business activities in the UK. These are described below. It is almost true to say that any sound business project is likely to be able to find appropriate finance, although it can still be difficult for start-up projects.

UK clearing banks

Clearing banks are willing to consider any proposition and have the ability to lend short-, medium- and long-term. Many of them have established separate divisions to service small businesses or to consider venture capital proposals.

They have the benefits of a wide UK network of branches and a deposit-taking capability. They have the bureaucratic disadvantage of size and arguably less understanding of the realities of business life.

The clearing banks themselves are not interested in anything other than lending on a commercial basis, usually against security.

Loan guarantee scheme
As part of the clearing bank lending arrangements should be considered the government loan guarantee scheme introduced in 1981. It is designed for start-up projects considered too risky by normal bank lending criteria. The lending bank is substantially protected against loss by government guarantee, the premium for which is a loading on the interest rate. The maximum loan subject to this arrangement is £75,000. Its continued existence is not certain.

Merchant banks
The 16 merchant banks comprising the Accepting Houses Committee tend to concentrate on large industrial and commercial lending. They do not take deposits from individuals and thus depend for their funds on borrowing in the money markets.

They all have corporate finance advisers and many of them have venture or development capital specialists.

They will consider equity and lending arrangements, although it is difficult to obtain finance from them for business start-ups (greenfield business). Their interest is much more in the provision of development capital, which may be syndicated. The clearing banks have specialist divisions which provide services similar to those of the merchant banks.

Members of the Issuing Houses Association
Members of the IHA can offer similar services to those of the merchant banks. Some of the Accepting Houses are also members of the IHA.

British Technology Group
BTG was formed to combine the resources of the National Enterprise Board (NEB) and the National Research Development Corporation (NRDC), with the object of promoting and developing technology in British industry by investing on a commercial basis in any size of company.

Exporting
The Government's Export Credits Guarantee Department was set up to guarantee approved foreign debts, thus reducing the risks involved in export debt collection.

Council for Small Industries in Rural Areas
The purpose of CoSIRA is to assist new business activity in rural areas in England. It is widely represented and in addition to making loans draws on the services of experienced businessmen to support manufacturing and service activities undertaken by businesses employing not more than 20 skilled workers.

Enterprise Zones
Special government financial assistance through the Department of the Environment is available in a number of areas which have been designated Enterprise Zones.

Management buy-outs

Many companies which offer corporate advisory services have specialists in the growing practice of management buy-outs who will assist managers to negotiate the purchase of a discrete business from a group of companies, and to arrange finance for the separate company and the acquisition by its management of a shareholding in it.

Venture capital

There is a substantial number of financial companies specialising in venture and development capital. The number has grown rapidly since the Finance Act 1983 introduced the Business Expansion Scheme (see below) on a far more realistic basis than the start-up scheme introduced in the previous year's Finance Act.

There are now about a hundred funds which are in the business of bringing together investors and fund-seekers and which offer professional investment advice.

Other sources of venture and development capital include the larger pension funds, the Scottish and Welsh Development Agencies, and foreign banks based in London. Investors in Industry plc (3i) (owned by the clearing banks) is estimated to have provided around 50 per cent of this type of finance; it also arranges funding from European sources.

Some of the funds concentrate their resources in limited areas, such as technology or oil. The British Steel Scheme, which has actively encouraged new business in the declining steel areas, must also be mentioned as an effective and successful source of finance.

The normal rules of financing are likely to be adapted to a higher gearing ratio for venture capital projects and start-ups. Equity and loan financing often go hand-in-hand to provide real rewards to financiers undertaking considerable risks. There may be a straight combination of the two and/or loans convertible into equity, and/or with preference shares, either redeemable or convertible.

The underlying aim in all cases is to motivate the management and provide the risk financier with attractive rewards for success.

Leasing

Many companies have taken advantage of opportunities to obtain fixed assets by leasing from a financier. Essentially it is just another method of borrowing and can be at favourable rates because the lessor has been able to take advantage of the relief through capital allowances (now at a reducing level), part of which may be passed on for the benefit of the lessee.

Debt factoring

A number of financial houses offer a debt factoring service which provides a company to which trade debts are owing with a more immediate source of funds. The service is usually available only in respect of UK debts and may be offered selectively, depending upon the quality of the debt portfolio. Most financial companies will act as factors only, with recourse to the assignor, but some trade as principals with no recourse.

This service does not cost a company significantly more than bank interest charges and it can greatly assist cash flow.

Business Expansion Scheme

This scheme offers considerable tax benefits to individuals with high tax rates.

Constraints on the investor are an upper annual limit of (at present) £40,000 and a requirement to retain the investment for not less than five years. The vast majority of individuals providing finance under the scheme are doing so through funding arrangements, but there is no reason why the investment cannot be made directly. The scheme's principal drawback is that the tax relief is not available to working directors.

Other government assistance

There is a very extensive range of financial assistance covering a wide field of applications arising from the Industrial Development Act 1982 and the Science and Technology Act 1965. Nearly all forms of assistance are conditional upon discretionary decisions by the appropriate government department and obtaining approval before committing the expenditure.

The following indicates the assistance available from various government departments, which offer help and advice on schemes within their own jurisdiction:

— projects considered to be in the national interest
— to assist export penetration
— research and development grants designed to assist in the modernisation of industry
  These include:
  — innovation of commercially marketable products
  — computer aided design and microprocessor applications
  — consultancy support for manufacturing
  — telecommunications
  — technology concerned with biotechnology, fibre optics and industrial robots
  — support of industrial research and development
— to improve transportation facilities
— the Youth Training Scheme
— to support development of computer skills
— to assist the development of tourism.

Many companies are not aware of the extensive nature of financial and other assistance available from the various government departments. Unfortunately, there is no centralised source of information and assistance, although there are a very limited number of publications fully classifying the schemes. They are worth study. The situation is dynamic and needs watching for new schemes being introduced from time to time.

Exit

Whenever an investment is made, it is sensible to consider how it can be realised. Minority interests, particularly if there is a controlling shareholding, are at a disadvantage. In an unquoted company, it will be difficult to find a buyer and with a minority interest, there will almost certainly be a heavy discount on realisation — perhaps 20 to 30 per cent.

In an unquoted company the Articles prescribe how shares may be transferred: usually there is provision for shares to be offered first pro rata to other shareholders in order to avoid disturbing the balance within the company which will have been carefully constructed. This is one way out, but it is a cumbersome procedure and artificial in determining the share price.

Alternatively, the company may be sold as a going concern, with or without shareholders retaining some of their interests. The following is an example of this course of action. A company in a service industry was sold on a multiple of the pre-tax profits not only for the year of sale, but also for the following year. As part of the deal the purchaser required that the top management be locked in with 20 per cent for a period of time to ensure a continuation in management commitment. Clearly there can be problems in a deal like this. To protect the second-year results the vendors insisted that all the members of the old board should retain control until the end of year two, joined by new members from the purchasing company. Provision also had to be made for business development costs to be treated in a special way to prevent short-term profits in the interests of the vendor being made at the expense of the purchaser's long-term interest. This deal worked satisfactorily for both parties.

Whether the intent is to sell to another operator or to seek a market quotation, probably on the Unlisted Securities Market, the requirements are similar:

- a proven management team
- a satisfactorily increasing profit record over two or three years, with a continuing trend forecast
- profit record preferably not dependent on a single product.

In the case of a sale of shareholdings there is no immediate benefit to the company. In the case of a market quotation, however, the main purpose may well be to bring new funds into the company by the issue of new shares. In the process, of course, a market is established, opening up the opportunity for the sale of shares when the time is right for an individual shareholder.

It should be noted that there are restrictions on the sale of shares acquired with the tax benefits of the Business Expansion Scheme or options under the Finance Act 1984.

The causes of business failure

A violent or sudden change in external circumstances beyond management control can be the cause of severe stress or even business failure, but the large majority of failures have to be attributed to management.

The principal causes of failure fall into five general categories: under-capitalisation, over-borrowing, over-trading, lax balance sheet control and unbalanced development projects.

Under-capitalisation

This arises from a failure fully to appreciate how success depends on having available the necessary funds. It occurs most frequently with new businesses. Funds to satisfy projected financial needs must be augmented by a generous contingency. It is never possible to forecast exactly what will happen, particularly in relation to turnover which has a very direct bearing on cash flow.

Over-borrowing

On p53 above, a number of key ratios were explained. One of those related to the gearing position. With the exception of certain venture capital situations, when loans may sometimes effectively be regarded as part of the capital structure, there are prudent ratios of borrowings to shareholders' capital and reserves, probably not exceeding 1:1 maximum.

Such ratios need to be calculated having regard to all company borrowings and company funding to be calculated in relation to tangible assets.

The impact of losses can rapidly cause a significant swing in the relative position of the funding sources.

Suppose a company position is as follows:

	£	Ratio
Borrowings	50,000	45
Net worth	60,000	55
Total funding	110,000	

Now assume losses of £15,000, which are funded by increasing the overdraft. Then the figures become:

	£	Ratio
Borrowings	65,000	59
Net worth	45,000	41
Total funding	110,000	

The situation is immediately serious. It can be expected that the bank will be monitoring the position regularly, probably against two or three criteria established in the borrowing agreements. A rapid deterioration as indicated is likely to result in an early meeting with the bankers!

An injection of new equity capital will, of course, have incremental borrowing benefits. If, in the above example, there is a new capital injection of £25,000, the position will be:

	£	Ratio
Borrowings	65,000	48
Net worth	70,000	52
Total funding	135,000	

This will support a further £5,000 of borrowing with a ratio of 1:1, therefore increasing total resources by £30,000.

Over-trading

Rapidly growing companies are especially vulnerable to cash difficulties. This is because working capital (debtors + stocks − creditors) increases in a more or less constant ratio to turnover. So there will be an ever increasing demand for finding working capital as turnover increases. This must be carefully planned and controlled if a cash crisis is to be avoided. One way of reducing the pressure is to arrange for debts to be factored, the cost of which will not be greatly in excess of bank interest rate. However, even if the debt portfolio is one the factor will accept, it is likely to be confined to UK debtors.

Different types of business have very different working capital requirements.

61

- cash businesses, such as the entertainment business. Requirements are minimal because of the absence of debtors and stocks.
- retail businesses, which normally have no debtors but must carry adequate stocks.
- service businesses. Financial activities and agencies have debtors but no trading stocks.
  Sales servicing activities carry spare parts which can, in some cases, be substantial.
- manufacturing has the most difficult problem, with debtors and stocks of raw materials, work in progress and finished goods. Even in well controlled businesses, these may amount to some 30 per cent of turnover.

Lax balance sheet control

If control over working capital components debtors, stocks and creditors temporarily loosens, within quite a short time cash flow can be under pressure. Debtors collected at 90 days average instead of 60 will increase cash requirements by some 8 or 9 per cent; stocks increasing from say 60 to 75 days by perhaps 3 or 4 per cent. An increased strain of, say, 12 per cent on a monthly turnover of £100,000 therefore requires additional capital of £12,000, and more if turnover is rising.

Unbalanced development projects

Even very large companies can find themselves in difficulty through undertaking development projects too risky in relation to total company resources. Such a situation can come about from a variety of causes:

- misjudgement of the financial consequences of undertaking such a significant project
- unforeseen deterioration in the net profitability of the business which must support the project through its development stages
- more costly development project than planned through, for example, technical difficulties which had not been contemplated, causing the project to be extended in time and/or increased manpower.
- slower market acceptance of the new product than expected.

Difficult development projects are most unlikely to proceed exactly as planned. The following rules should apply:

- not undertaking a project which, given adverse circumstances, could jeopardise the total business, however attractive the rewards may seem
- ensuring that there is adequate resource cover even for a 'worst case' projection
- evaluating in advance the sensitivity of the various components in the project
- ensuring strong project management and overall board control through cash releases only against the achievement of defined stages in the development project.

Chapter 4

The Business Plan

The preparation of a business plan is a prerequisite of controlled business operation, whatever the size of company and regardless of whether there is an external funding requirement. In forming the plan, preparatory work has to be done, investigations made, options considered and decisions taken in a number of key areas. The resulting work can then be brought together into a comprehensive document, prepared by the managing director, for approval by the board.

Chapter 1 established the need for a clear definition of the business the company intends to be in, so that it can focus on the right area of the market and adopt the best methods of serving that market.

The second aspect which needs early and careful consideration is the key objectives of the company. These may be few in number but are fundamental to the development of the business. There must be agreement on the objectives, and once this has been achieved, they should be kept firmly in view and not changed unless or until they are proved incapable of achievement, in which case new objectives must be established.

The next consideration is the strategy by which the objectives are to be achieved and the timescale. Within the broad strategy is a series of tactical action plans.

The business plan needs to span a period of time, usually, from three to five years. In some cases, particularly in a capital intensive business, a longer view may have to be taken because long lead times are necessary for planning, developing and commissioning complicated buildings and plant. The longer the time span, however, the less reliable will be the calculations. It is usual to plan in considerable detail for the financial year immediately ahead – the budget year. For the following periods the plan should be clear about the main thrusts of the business and should attempt reasonable financial forecasts. While these forecasts are unlikely to prove accurate, they are very valuable in forming long-term plans and strategies.

Changes are occurring continually in any business and its environment, so plans must be regularly reviewed if they are to retain credibility. The usual practice is to roll forward the plan each each year and, in the process of doing so, compare carefully what actually happened with what was intended to happen. With experience, business plans gradually become more credible.

A business plan is prepared by management for management. It should not be determined by financial people, although it would be incomplete without their contribution.

Accounting information

To construct a sound business plan basic records are required from which to work.

Plans prepared for any new business will be looked at in the knowledge that they must be based to a fair extent on assumptions and intentions.

The minimum requirements are:

- an accurate and timely record of transactions
- grouping transactions into meaningful accounts
- regular and timely information for management
- understanding fixed and variable costs and break-even (Chapter 3)
- the ability to determine profit contributions for each product/service/activity (Chapter 3).

There must also be sufficient information concerning market and cost trends to make reasoned business forecasts.

Key issues

Before preparing a business plan, there are some key issues which must be addressed. In summary they are:

1. Determine the objectives of the investors.
2. Analyse the historic business performance to date.
3. Identify those factors which are essential to success in the chosen market.
4. Determine quite objectively the strengths and weaknesses of the existing business.
5. Evaluate the opportunities which could be available, and the competitive threats, in a changing environment.

With the situation thus appraised, identify the options and the risks, and evaluate each of them: then build the plan to secure the objectives. This chapter considers how.

Corporate objectives

Deciding the objectives of the company is fundamental because all else flows from them. They are likely to include:

- the aimed for position of the company in its market (or market sectors) and market share(s)
- the extent to which the company intends to develop into other business activities or related markets
- if and when the company intends to seek quotation on the Stock Exchange, or otherwise to open up the 'exit' route for shareholders
- the planned rate of growth for, usually, three to five years ahead. It is not enough to say, for example, that the company will grow at 50 per cent per annum without also saying how this is to be measured. It is probably best to measure 'net profit before tax excluding extraordinary items'. Or growth could be defined in terms of 'earnings per share'.
- methods of financing and constraints, including intended ratios of borrowings to shareholders' funds and the intended rate of turnover of operating assets.

More or less detail can be included, but it is usually best to state a few, clearly defined goals. They must make a coherent package; for example, if a stock market quotation is sought, the growth plans must be such as will support that objective.

It is a useful discipline also to decide what you do *not* intend to do. The value lies in forcing management positively to justify any intended departure from policy. If, for example, you are in the business of free magazine distribution, you may well establish that the company does not intend to seek distribution through the newsagency channels, because of the fundamentally different methods and financial implications entailed.

The planning process

A business plan sets out the methods by which it is intended to achieve the corporate objectives. It emerges from a planning process which is likely to include the following steps: first, considering the many factors relevant to the achievement of the objectives, and assessing each of them; second, identifying the options which are open to the business, and evaluating each of them; and third, deciding which course of action to take. In evaluating the options, one particular course often becomes obvious as the right one to take. If it does not, either the managing director must make the decision, or the alternative plans with their likely consequences must be put up for decision by the board.

The board may wish to keep control of the situation and the commitment of financial resources by requiring the plan to be developed in phases, only approving the release of further resources when key checkpoints have been satisfactorily reached.

Development of the business plan should be considered as a two-way exercise: downwards from top management and upwards from those responsible for detailed implementation.

'Top-down' planning

The 'top-down' plan, as it is frequently referred to, is senior management's expression of its intentions over a three- to five-year planning period. It entails establishing the key objectives, and the annual rate at which it is intended the business shall grow. It is unlikely to be a consensus document. Its purpose is to construct a model of the business as it is planned to be, establishing the key ratios and the assumptions underlying them. Among other things, it includes the construction of projected balance sheets and financial requirements. Estimates or projections beyond three years are likely to be inaccurate, but they are valuable in establishing important indications of opportunities and problems likely to arise. For example, in the planning of overseas markets, production facilities and new products, long lead times are almost always required. The real value of the work lies in the discussions and studies which are an essential part of the planning process.

It is most important that the will of the board and senior management is respected throughout the organisation. Once the decisions have been taken and the policy has been determined, the time for discussion is over: the whole team must act coherently to achieve the intended goals.

'Bottom-up' planning

The second part of the process is to build the plan from 'bottom up', incorporating considerable detail. In larger organisations, those managers who will be responsible for achieving the results are involved in the planning. Their commitment gives the plan its credibility. The 'bottom-up' process has special relevance to the preparation of the coming year's annual plan and budget. If the bottom-up plan turns out to be significantly different from the top-down model, those differences and the reasons for them have to be established and considered. It is acceptable, however, for there to be a reasonable gap between the top-down and bottom-up versions, because top management should consistently be seeking to stretch the organisation.

Once the budget for the coming year has been established, it becomes a key navigational aid, against which all subsequent monitoring will take place. The budget is the financial expression of the company's plan for that year, and it has to carry the agreement of senior managers who are to be held responsible for its implementation.

It is therefore most desirable for these personnel to be involved in the planning process, agree with the decisions and be committed to successful implementation. If this does not happen problems are almost inevitable, because no worthwhile manager will take responsibility for a plan unless he believes he can succeed with it, and that the resources given to him are adequate.

Business models

A third and most useful technique is to construct a financial model of the business, preferably by using a computer. The model can then be examined to discover the financial consequences of making different planning assumptions. 'What if' questions are necessary in most business situations. Without a computer they are slow and difficult calculations to make and will therefore often not be attempted. The construction of a financial model of the business is concerned with ratios. It is therefore necessary to know, or assume, what the key ratios are. This technique is most useful in the preparation of a 'top-down' business plan (see p65).

Implementing the business plan

Successful implementation of plans is difficult — far more difficult than the drafting of plans on paper. Much depends on how members of the team work together. Examples abound of what can be achieved with a top, well co-ordinated management team firmly led by a determined managing director. And vice versa!

There are two key requirements. First, to ensure the whole organisation is facing in the same direction, committed to achieving the corporate goals. Second, the timely availability of information concerning the company's performance, including, of course, financial reports drawn in such a way as to provide each level of management with everything it needs to know. (More consideration is given to the monitoring of performance in Chapter 7.)

A plan should not be rigid. It is a means to an end. In this case, the end is the achievement of the objectives. Flexibility of method is therefore vital. If it becomes clear that circumstances have changed, or that certain actions are not proving successful, something must be done about it. And the sooner the better. The ability to make quick and appropriate adjustments comes from careful monitoring of the plan, particularly those factors which have been identified as being fundamental to successful achievement.

It is sensible to try to anticipate how events might vary from the plan, to think through possible reactions to changed circumstances, and to prepare contingency plans. These will be of great assistance to management when having to decide, under the pressure of events, what actions need to be taken.

Framework of the business plan

The plan should be developed along the following general lines:

1. Introduction: historical background and financial situation. Brevity is valuable, but this introductory section must be comprehensive and highlight the key issues leading to the preparation of the plan.
2. The business mission: a statement of the business in which the company is perceived to operate and its intentions in the chosen field
3. Corporate objectives (as discussed above)
4. Marketing analysis and plans
5. Sales plan
6. Operational plan
7. Technical plan
8. Manpower plan
9. Organisation plan
10. Financial plan
11. Information and control
12. Contingency plans.

The marketing concept

Profitably servicing a market is the fundamental purpose of any business. Satisfying the consumer is the beginning and the end of marketing. It is the process by which the management must identify, anticipate and satisfy the wants of the customer — and do it on a profitable basis.

Some important aspects of marketing are:

— putting the customer first, all the time
— product innovation
— uniqueness
— design and identification
— value for money (quality at the price)
— product branding or marking
— packaging and recognition
— communication.

It has been said that the function of marketing is to deliver the right product, at the right price, at the right time, in the right place, at the required profit contribution.

In a broader sense, marketing represents an attitude of mind in relation to the customer. It is not the prerogative of one person or department. It is the very soul of the enterprise and, as such, all departments and all employees within the organisation should be directed and trained to take their part in it. The telephonist, receptionist, service engineer and accountant, to take just four random examples, are all important elements in establishing the attitude of the business to its customers. Regrettably few UK businesses comprehend this basic truth. This is evidenced by the dissatisfaction among customers which is so widespread, not least among the nationalised industries.

It has to be understood from boardroom to shopfloor and constantly re-inforced. Successful business is about discipline and constant attention to detail in every respect: faulty implementation of sound market planning can be, and usually is, fatal.

For every business the essential question is the same: can the business attract and satisfy enough customers to generate the volume of revenues needed to cover all the operating costs, service the interest and other financing costs, depreciate the fixed assets, set aside sufficient sums to ensure the future development of the business and provide a satisfactory return on capital invested?

The business manager, then, seeks properly to understand the market he aims to serve and its dynamic nature. Not until he has done that will he be able to assess the opportunities it offers, to design his products or services to satisfy it on a profitable basis, and ensure that new product developments maintain or increase his share of it.

'Marketing' and 'selling'

This is an appropriate place to sort out the confusion which often exists between the two terms: 'marketing' and 'selling'. They describe two quite different functions.

Marketing is the process by which the management identifies, anticipates and satisfies the requirements of the customer on a profitable basis. The function embraces the design and development of products intended to achieve the company's objectives in the market; the positioning of these products in the market; the overall planning for their introduction; pricing policies; the advertising, promotion and PR work required to achieve penetration; packaging and present-ation; ensuring customer satisfaction by establishing principles and standards of post-sales servicing; ensuring that financial objectives are satisfied.

This conceptual work is not done in a vacuum, but by working closely with other departments in the business to ensure practical solutions and commitment to achieve them. In those senses, marketing is a staff rather than a line function, and in smaller companies may well be the responsibility of the managing director himself, for it clearly goes to the core of the business activity.

The sales function is that of implementing and achieving the marketing plans and objectives. This requires quite different skills. Marketing plans, however soundly based, are likely to prove ineffective if the sales function is not drawn closely and enthusiastically into the work, and believes marketing policies and plans are well founded. This is the only way to achieve commitment to succeed. The head of sales often reports to the head of marketing; but this need not be the case, and it is probably preferable for each to report directly to the managing director.

Analysis of the market

The starting point when looking at any business proposition must be an analysis of the market and the position of the company's products in it — currently and within the next several years. For products whose specialised nature and low volume make any overall market assessments less relevant, some of the wider studies can be ignored; but it is still absolutely necessary to understand the trends and technical developments taking place if the company is to remain competitive in its chosen sector.

Points about the overall market which need to be understood include:

- the different sectors into which the overall market should be classified. This is very important, because it is really to each individual sector, with its particular characteristics, that the company must address itself. Most references to 'market' indicate those individual sectors or gaps — niche markets — in which, though relatively small, the company has a chance to become dominant and to have a good deal of control. The identification of such opportunities is very important.
- the general size of the market, its trends and rates of growth (or decline)
- the shape of the market, eg its constituent parts, geographical spread, age profile, socio-economic composition and so on
- the extent to which the market is price sensitive, ie is it 'elastic' in the sense that significant volume changes are likely to take place in response to price movements?
- the competitive elements seeking a place in the market, both UK and foreign, and their relative strengths and weaknesses. The characteristics and benefits of each product must be established and compared with competitive products. The best methods of exploiting and reinforcing the strong product characteristics and of avoiding damage arising from weakness can then be worked out.
- The most significant competitors, the market leaders, tend to determine much of what happens in the market. They have the initiative and can influence factors such as timing to strengthen their position.
- the probability and nature of technical developments. An outstanding example is the manner in which the products of the computer industry have, year after year, achieved quite remarkable real cost reductions and power increases.
- the changing pattern of distribution within the market: for example, the trend towards more direct servicing of major national accounts by the manufacturers, the reduced influence of the wholesaler and the demise of many of the smaller retail outlets. Or again, the relocation from town centre to out-of-town sites with large selling areas and adjacent car parking facilities.

Knowledge of the market can never be complete at any point in time. The pursuit of great accuracy is frequently just not worth the time and cost involved. But enough information must be secured, and it must be secured on a continuing basis. Much of the input can be collected through the routine sales activities of the company itself and from carefully analysing company data, guarantee cards and service records. This can be supplemented from generally available external sources, such as regular contacts with suppliers, trade literature, Chambers of Commerce and government departments. Some more specific professionally conducted research of the market may also be needed. This may be relatively cheap and founded on 'desk' research backed up by a limited number of interviews; or it may be a quite expensively conducted in-depth enquiry.

The idea of using formal market research often meets with resistance from those who claim it will be irrelevant to a product or company as different as theirs. But this is not so. Market research will, at the very least, serve to confirm beliefs about the market situation: indeed it would be very surprising for experienced operators if the analysis provided a mass of information that was not already known. But the fine tuning, the correct positioning of a product, needs accurate data, professionally compiled and analysed. Asking the correct questions of the right sample of interviewees is a highly skilled task.

Writing the brief upon which the research work is based is an important job done by management, with help from the researcher. If the brief is not sound, the response will be unreliable.

It should be said that even after excellent briefing, market research can produce unreliable results. This is most likely to happen if the research subjects are conceptual, or not within the previous experience of the interviewee. For example, the early UK research into intentions to use office photo copiers using ordinary paper was discouraging. It was also ignored! The proposition (at that time) of not selling the photo copying machines, but of renting them on a usage basis, was novel. It also turned out to be a brilliant marketing concept. The more revolutionary the concept, the more difficult it is to research.

The marketing plan

The assembly of information and its analysis thus completed, the marketing plan can be prepared which will address the following:

- product objectives, for example:

Product A: To secure market leadership by increasing sector penetration in year 1 from 10 to 15 per cent and within the following two years to 25 per cent.

Product B: To improve market share by increasing sector penetration in year 1 from 3 to 5 per cent and to 10 per cent by the end of year 3.

Product C: To hold market share at 3 per cent and to plan withdrawal by the end of year 3.

Product D: To introduce new product D at the beginning of Q3 and secure a firm base for expansion to achieve penetration of 10 per cent by year 3.

Product E: To develop a new product E to be ready to offer commercially by the commencement of year 2.

- phasing the development of the market penetration. For example, it may not be thought practical to seek a national market in the initial stages. The method by which market penetration will be achieved, and at what speed, must be stated. The decision may be to spread out into the main conurbations in a series of waves, thus allowing market proving at the same time. TV areas may be a very important factor in the strategy.
- establishing the targeted order intake, stock policies, order backlog and sales volumes for each product at determined prices and margins.
- defining the distribution channels to be employed and the transport arrangements
- determining the sales methods, eg wholesalers, agencies and dedicated sales force, and its organisation
- establishing the priority to be attached to international development, and the methods to be adopted
- advertising and promotion policies
- after-sales servicing policies

— the corporate design and communication policies.

This is not intended as a comprehensive checklist, but an indication of the nature of the decisions which must be taken in order to assemble a credible marketing plan.

Product planning

A business sells either goods or services. Or both. The marketing plan is concerned with the methods by which these 'products' are effectively and profitably sold in the markets addressed. Therefore the most important influence on product characteristics, design innovation, packaging and profitability must emanate from the marketing function. This key aspect needs more detailed consideration.

A convenient starting point in determining product policies might be to identify the different opportunities which the market presents. Each kind of approach has very different problems and must be handled in a particular way. The broad categories of product policy can be summarised thus:

— market penetration: selling an existing product into an existing market
— market development: selling an existing product into a new market
— product development: selling a new product into an existing market
— diversification: selling a new product into a new market.

The correct positioning of the product in its chosen sector is also essential. The thorough analysis of that market and the characteristics and benefits of the particular product should lead the company to identify its best opportunity for success. For example:

— which target customers?
— what advertising to reach them?
— which market support services will be necessary?
— what pricing policy?
— what distribution method?
— with what financial implications?

The company will always be looking for some discernible attribute which will give the product a unique advantage. Because markets are dynamic, market advantage is likely to last for only a short period before the competition reacts by matching and improving its own products. This makes life uncomfortable for the supplier, but is to the great advantage of the customer. Consumer benefits of this kind occur readily in an unrestricted market and may not exist at all under monopoly conditions.

The company will also be seeking security. Investment in product development and launching is frequently heavy. Protection of that investment, and full exploitation of it, will be a constant aim. Security may be sought by achieving a leading position in the chosen market or by product branding. Another source of security may be found in patent protection.

The decision whether or not to rely on patent protection, with consequent public disclosure, will depend on many considerations. It can provide real security in the market-place for some years, but the company which holds such a patent must seek constantly to improve and build on its original patent base so that 'building round the patent' by competitors becomes increasingly difficult. It was by these methods, combined with its rental policy, that Xerox secured a leading position in the international market for many years: it was only brought to an end by the threat of American anti-trust legislation.

Most products have an economic life cycle. The portfolio of products will therefore consist of old products declining and new products rising to take their place or to develop the product range. A new product development programme is therefore essential to success.

Review of the company's products, proposed improvements and new developments in priority order must take place regularly, together with progress monitoring of the necessary design and production work, and assessment of the competitive situation. This is a proper matter for senior management and board attention.

Of course, in designing new products, consideration must be given not only to the current situation but to the situation which it is anticipated will exist when the product is introduced; this must be some years ahead, and is very unlikely to be less than a year ahead. In fast moving markets — electronics, for instance — that is a long time.

Appendix 4 outlines the basic approach to designing and marketing a new product. It is derived from an actual case involving the development of a new product for a market which did not offer much scope for innovation or uniqueness. The end result justified the careful preparatory work which took place over a period of about a year. First there was a careful study of the market sector to be addressed. Then a brief as to the product characteristics required and the indicated sales price which it would be necessary to achieve. In this particular case, consumer panels were formed under the guidance of a professional researcher to discover consumer reactions to pre-production models of the product, before designs were finally approved and frozen.

While some of the stages apply particularly to a new product, others apply to existing products, whose positioning needs constant and regular review.

Two points are worth emphasising. The first concerns product design. It is essential to give full attention from the beginning to the attractiveness of the product as it will be presented to the market-place. It must clearly be functional, but that is not enough on its own. Simplicity is a key principle in product design. The second point concerns cost. Detailed thought must be given to 'designing out' unnecessary costs by simplifying design to minimise the complexity of the manufacturing process. This makes quality control significantly easier to maintain, and without quality control to a very high standard opportunities in the market-place can never be properly exploited. Many UK manufacturing and service businesses have apparently still to learn this lesson.

The sales plan

Detailed proposals to implement the marketing plan can now be prepared. These will, of course, reflect the breakdown of the business into the chosen market sectors.

The sales management will be concerned with the following main elements:

 — order intake
 — gross margins
 — order backlog
 — invoiced sales.

The margins on different products and market sectors are very unlikely to be the same. The product mix is therefore important in achieving the overall margin required from the sales function.

The order intake and backlog are both fundamental. The backlog relates to firm orders received but which, at any given date, have not been executed. This provides a necessary cushion in the planning of supply sourcing and an underpinning of future sales forecasts. On the other hand, too long a delivery time may not be an advantage — the customer may be unhappy or unwilling to wait that long. The size of the backlog for each product and market sector is therefore a matter for careful judgement.

An expanding business naturally expects an increasing order backlog in absolute terms: the ratio to future sales turnover, however, may reflect a policy intent. If the policy is to aim for an increased ratio then, other things being equal, the orders available for current invoicing will be reduced, as illustrated in Figure 4.1.

	£	Ratio to forecast sales	Projected turnover
Opening backlog	2,000	25%	8,000
Orders received in period	750		
	2,750		
Target backlog increase 1% per month	2,080	26%	
Available for invoicing	670		

Figure 4.1. *Calculating orders available for current invoicing*

If sales themselves are planned to be increased there will be considerable pressure to achieve the required increase in order intake.

	£
Assume fixed operating costs	50,000
Assume expected gross margin 40%, break-even turnover required	125,000
If margins are eroded to 37.5%, break-even turnover must rise to	133,000
Now, suppose planned turnover is	200,000
At gross margin 40%	80,000
Less fixed costs	50,000
Profit	30,000
But, if margins are reduced to 37.5% yielding	75,000
Less fixed costs	50,000
Profit	25,000
Consequential reduction in profit from a margin reduction equivalent to 6.25% (ie 2.5% on 40%)	5,000
The effect on planned profit, however, is no less than 16.6% reduction or, put the other way round, to achieve the planned profit of £30,000 to justify the margin reduction, sales must be increased to	£213,000

Figure 4.2. *Importance of the sales margin*

The second critical element is the sales margin. The wish to achieve orders makes it tempting for sales representatives to offer prices which will reflect reduced margins. There must therefore be a very firm policy about margin control, limiting discretion for price discounting. The importance of this can be illustrated in Figure 4.2. The monitoring of the position is a key control for management, and is further considered in Chapter 7.

Because the sales plan is inevitably more concerned with the first year of the business plan, it will be dealt with more appropriately in Chapter 5.

The longer range sales plan should be particularly concerned with organisation and structure of the sales team year by year and the likely numbers and types of the sales representation required to meet the intended sales targets, both at home and internationally. From this, it will be possible to consider the nature of the problems which will have to be solved. In particular, in a rapidly growing business of increasing complexity, the availability and quality of the sales management will receive special consideration. Costing of the sales activity for each year can then be compared with the ratio allocated in the total business model: if there is a serious discrepancy, the proposals will need further study.

Example

Let us assume a business growing from £1m to £3m turnover over three years, excluding inflation, as follows:

	Base year	Year 1	Year 2	Year 3
Turnover £m	1	1.7	2.5	3
Index	100	170	250	300

Average sales capability per sales person is £100,000 per annum. For new staff, six months must be allowed to reach that level, during which period a sales capability of £50,000 is assumed. Allowing for differing engagement periods, it is calculated that sales staff will build up as follows:

	Base year	Year 1	Year 2	Year 3
Number of sales staff	11	21	27	32
Number of managers	1	2	2	3
Sales support staff, say, at 30% of selling staff	3	7	9	11
Total staff	15	30	38	46
Basic salaries				
Sales staff, say	150	240	360	442
Managerial	25	40	50	65
Support staff, say	18	30	48	60
Total basic	193	310	458	567

	Base year	Year 1	Year 2	Year 3
Total basic	193	310	458	567
Commission at 5%	50	85	125	150
Other employment costs, say 20% of basic	39	62	92	113
Total employment cost	282	457	675	830
Ratio to turnover %	28	27	27	28
Company model for sales staff employment %	25	25	25	25

This example indicates that sales management must review the detailed composition of the employment budget with a view to seeking a reduction of 2 to 3 per cent each year. There are clearly several methods which should be considered to improve the effectiveness of the sales performance.

The operations plan

This task can be broken down into two elements:

- product development
- supply sourcing.

Product development

Consideration of the marketing issues above drew attention to the need for products to react to changes in the market. Reaction may be to adapt the product to new customer requirements by fairly simple improvements or upgrading. Or it may take the form of product innovation or development.

The most careful planning is required to ensure the future business position is protected, and this task may well be assigned to a separate functional unit. This unit should logically report to the marketing function. There has at least to be a strong marketing influence at every stage. Design, packaging, engineering, production and finance all have a part to play in achieving the most appropriate product.

This matter is so important to the future trading position that the board must be involved in approving the brief for product plans and monitoring their achievement on a regular basis.

Product sourcing

Product demand has been determined by the sales plan. Two things are now needed. First, the stockholding policies. Those concerned with servicing the market will be determined by the marketing and sales plans. Those concerned with the production process will be decided on by that function, assuming that the business is to manufacture its own supplies. Raw materials stocks will be influenced by the supply location and time required to bring it to the factory, the availability of alternative sources, and the duration of the production process.

A fundamental board decision will be whether to make or buy. This may apply to the whole product or to its sub-assemblies. If the whole sourcing programme is external, manufacturing problems are avoided, but this advantage may be partly counterbalanced by some loss of control. However, there are many examples of soundly based decisions to source externally and still achieve control, through the purchaser's close involvement with the supplier's production process. Even when the sourcing is 'in house' manufacture, it is very seldom that all the necessary parts will be built internally. Many, perhaps most or even all, will be bought in for assembly.

Whatever the policy, it is of paramount importance that product quality criteria are clearly defined by the board, and that a system exists to ensure that that product quality is achieved. This point cannot be over-emphasised. There are, of course, many factors affecting the achievement of the required quality. Setting the standards, insisting on their being achieved, and training the people are the three principles which should be observed without compromise. While the problem of quality achievement and maintenance is more widely recognised in the UK now than used to be the case, and has clearly been solved by some companies, there is certainly a long way to go before the overall quality of product, work and services in this country reaches competitive international standards. This applies equally to businesses in the export market and those competing against imports into the UK.

With sourcing planned, the first cross check can be made to establish product costs and thus product margins. If the required margin is not there, more detailed work is necessary, bearing in mind of course that product costs will be significantly affected by volume. This is a good example of the iterative process which is a necessary and valuable part of the planning process.

The interplay of product costs and product pricing is therefore a very critical area for examination, and several alternative models may have to be considered before deciding on the formulae likely to yield the optimum margin results.

This points to the need for good financial advice from an early date. Many entrepreneurs do not appreciate this need and are reluctant to pay for it. The difficulty in a small business is that the accountant in professional practice can seldom satisfy management's requirement for timely information to assist in making decisions about the future; and a full-time financial manager may not be justified. A solution might well be found in the employment on a part-time basis of a skilled management accountant. He would have the necessary experience and, given a good recording system, he would only need to be available a few days a month, which the business should be able to afford. With a bit of luck he would have a small computer to speed the work along and be able to help the client to introduce at an early date a computer of his own.

The manpower plan

It will now be possible to put together a manpower plan, phasing the introduction of directors, supervisors, managers and other employees to satisfy the operational plans. The key elements are:

- matching the manpower requirements by skill and category
- ensuring there is a proper description of each job and a profile of the qualities needed to satisfy its satisfactory performance
- a well planned system of selection and recruitment
- a well planned system for training and development.

In a rapidly growing business, the manpower lead time can represent a significant investment before revenue results cover the costs. It may well take six months before a salesman is properly effective.

As personnel increase in number, more senior management may also be required. This not only represents a significant cost, but also usually requires a substantial lead time. There should be a strong bias towards internal development, and existing employees must be carefully screened before the search goes outside, but it is important not to appoint managers who cannot reasonably be expected to succeed. If external recruitment is necessary, there should be a proper search for the skills and experience required. It will be at least six months before the recruitment process is completed and the new manager has been able to get himself released from his previous employment. It is generally good advice not to be strongly guided by 'personal contacts' until other applicants are available for comparative assessment.

The appointment of managers is a key task and fundamental to the success of the business; it is more important than any other factor. The managing director needs to know exactly what he is looking for, what the job to be done really is and what foreseeable demands will be put on the new manager. Recruitment should take place against a job profile which identifies the important characteristics needed for good performance. However careful the selection process, some accidents are bound to happen which can be very damaging to the company and demoralising to employees. But with careful attention, mistakes can be minimised.

More detailed consideration is given to this most important matter in Chapter 8.

The technical plan

Now is the time for the technical support to be considered. Much of this is the province of the engineer, be he mechanical or electrical, or both. The future technical capability of the business must figure high on the priority list, and there must be plans in place to:

- monitor external technological trends
- develop technical solutions in response to management briefs
- specify systems requirements and applications
- initiate proposals to management.

Such considerations are as relevant to the service business as to the manufacturer. It may well be the case that professional external advice is required to support in-house capability.

Developments in other advanced countries, particularly the USA and Japan, must be regularly monitored. There are signs of advanced electronic solutions being developed for integrated transaction, communication, design and production systems. Within the next 20 years these will almost certainly be significantly improving competitive capability. The UK simply has to be able to match this technical progress.

The other element to be considered is that of space — the provision of appropriately located office, warehouse, showroom and factory facilities. The three- to five-year planning process is essential when it comes to ensuring that the company has the right kind and the right amount of space. Professional design, ergonomic and system skills will play important parts in the space planning programme.

The balance between the immediate need for space and the potential requirement in, say, three years' time is critical. Moving is a most expensive and disruptive business. On the other hand, carrying excessive dead space is also expensive. With some luck, and forward planning, adjacent space may provide room for expansion and it is something which can be checked out before commitments are made. Sometimes, if the need for significant factory expansion is anticipated, it is possible to acquire land – or better, perhaps, a lease – and to develop and plan in logical stages as demand can be more accurately foreseen. This kind of development can be very successful, but it has to be envisaged right at the beginning, so that the architect and engineer can plan long-term satisfactory layouts.

The organisation and control plan

It is important to plan how the business will be controlled as it develops, especially if it is growing, or is expected to grow, fast. In a fairly small organisation, for example, the managing director is likely to perform the role of the marketing function, with a sales manager responsible for getting the orders. As the organis-ation grows in complexity, pressures will increase for the managing director to be involved in the search for new products and markets, more travel, financial control and so on. A marketing manager may have to be appointed and, if this is not the sales manager, there may be conflict. This problem should be anticipated. Moving from a small operation to a medium-sized business, and then to a large business, involves very considerable stress. Indeed, it requires great changes in attitude and in the methods by which the business is run. It is often the case that the necessary adaptations are beyond the capability of the original entrepreneurs. Planning methods of control for the future are therefore vital – and another reason why non-executive directors can play an important role.

By way of example, Figure 4.3 shows how a rapidly growing business could move through structural phases over a five- to seven-year period. This example illustrates the rapidly changing role of the players: it also illustrates that, when recruiting new personnel, some view must be taken of the likely changes in the tasks to be performed so that development potential is assessed at the time of recruitment.

Organisation is about effective control, and this depends largely on having the right information at the right time. Communications plans are therefore also important and are dealt with below (p81).

The financial plan

With the work done so far, the plan can now be translated into financial terms. This is where the accountant's role is most important, not just as one who prepares sets of figures, but as a communicator.

It has to be accepted that functional managers are primarily concerned with the effective performance of their main tasks. This nearly always involves some understanding of figures, but in many cases this understanding is so limited that financial information is not used properly or is rejected altogether. It is up to the accountant, therefore, to present information in terms understandable to the recipient, and to communicate effectively – to explain simply the message of the figures and take time to evaluate the information with the manager concerned.

This does not always happen and, instead, a gap opens between the finance function and the business managers, each party tending to be suspicious of

Phase I

Phase II — say, within two or three years

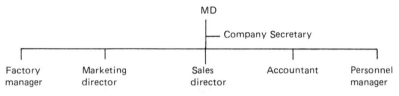

Phase III — say, within another two or three years

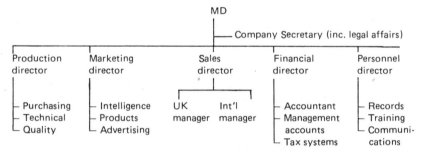

Figure 4.3. *Changes in structure of a rapidly growing business over a five- to seven-year period*

the other. It is a part of the accountant's role to be realistic and objective and when the inevitable differences in attitude emerge between, say, him and the marketing staff, the best overall result will undoubtedly occur if these differences are recognised and respected. The planning process is in fact an excellent way to bring about good working relationships.

The basic financial package comprises the following:

- profit and loss accounts
- balance sheets
- cash flows
- funding statement.

Profit and loss account
This is intended to match revenues with the costs incurred in their earning. The projected profit and loss account is prepared by monthly periods for the first year of the plan (the budget year), by quarters for the second year and annually or half-yearly for subsequent years.

Comparative figures are shown for the last completed financial year (as a minimum), together with projected results for the current year (because the plan will be put together during the latter part of that year with the final results then unknown).

The profit and loss account should include a summary of the order intake and sales projections, by product and by market sector.

Because there is a great deal of detail involved in keeping accounting records, the important figures must be highlighted so that the reader gets the message clearly and does not have to search for what he needs. It is necessary to bring out clearly:

- net revenues
- cost of sales
- gross margin
- variable expenses
- contribution
- fixed overhead expenses.

It is convenient to group the overheads into related categories, such as:

- Selling expenses: sales staff employment costs — salaries, commissions, bonuses, pensions and national insurance contributions; travel expenses; advertising and promotional costs
- General and administrative: head office costs, insurances, general management employment costs and related expenses
- Financial: expenses such as interest on borrowings, perhaps depreciation (although it clearly affects production costs), professional fees
- Research and development: If grants are receivable, these are best identified with this cost and deducted from it. Care is needed in the accounting for licence income; it may be appropriate to include it under this heading or as part of sales revenues, depending on its nature.

The advantages of so arranging matters are:

- to improve control and enable comparisons to be more easily made
- to relate subheadings of expenses to revenues, where ratios for each can be established in the overall planning process and more easily compared with the business financial model.

Overhead expenses are well named. They have to be carried out of the 'contribution'. The effective organisation and control of overheads is therefore vital. They tend to build up and are difficult to reduce. Each cost must be justified and alternative methods of achieving the desired result considered. Most overheads are about employing staff, and the oncost arising from employment — directly, such as national insurance contributions and pension costs, and indirectly, in the demands on space and facilities. 'Only if we really must' is the appropriate guideline for incurring overheads.

The importance of understanding the nature of fixed costs in relation to the revenue break-even point, and profitability, was illustrated above (p49). The changing break-even requirement should figure in the financial reporting package every period.

The annual planning process should re-examine the structure of overhead costs, and not start from the assumption that the existing level is necessarily correct.

Balance sheet

The plan will forecast the balance sheet position during and at the end of the planning period.

It is desirable to have a forecast balance sheet to coincide with the end of each period for which the profit and loss account has been prepared. There should at least be quarterly balance sheets for the first two years and annual ones thereafter.

The balance sheet must above all focus on the amount and make-up of current assets, because of their importance in relation to liquidity and their demands on resources when a business is growing. Chapter 6 examines this in greater detail.

Cash flow statements
The profit and loss account has to be reflected in cash terms by the construction of cash flow statements coinciding with the same periods as the profit plan. These statements will reveal the funding requirements of the business. Management must then consider the feasibility of satisfying the funding needed. There is a variety of sources available, as discussed above (p56). If the plans are too ambitious and causing too great a strain on financial capability, however, there is no alternative but to return to the planning table and consider ways in which the business can cut its coat according to its cloth: or to consider whether some more fundamental policy may have to be contemplated (such as seeking a merger with another company or new capital injection).

An operational plan without its financial implications as set out above, is gravely deficient. It should not be acceptable to management: it will not be acceptable to either bankers or investors.

The communications plan

Very few businesses set out to make a communications plan. And yet it is of the greatest importance. A business will not achieve its potential if deliberate steps are not taken to ensure good, smooth communication of information and ideas. For this reason it is worth while assigning communication policy to a main board director.

There are two categories of communication: external and internal. External communication includes:

- trading relationships
- customers
- collection of operating data (eg market, technical)
- shareholders
- financial markets/sources.

Internal communication includes:

- downward movement of operational information
- upward movement of operational information
- dissemination of business philosophy and objectives
- financial information and progress
- control information
- personnel policies.

The communications plan should take into account:

- the importance of design throughout the communication process in reflecting the character and style of the organisation
- the use of audio and visual aids both externally and internally

— electronic and computer technology which will play an ever more important part in communication. Chapter 9 deals with this matter more fully, but the concept of the 'paperless' office is no longer futuristic. The trend towards total office systems is already with us.

The contingency plan

The considerable amount of work involved in preparing a realistic and credible business plan will by now be evident. It can only be done with a belief in its necessity and a great effort of will to achieve. The target must be to get the plan in place before the financial year starts.

Having completed the plan, it is most valuable to analyse those parts of it which may expose the business to particular risks, and to evaluate them. This analysis should form part of the plan, and whenever possible there should be an outline of the financial consequences and contemplated counteraction.

Some elements of the plan will have overriding influence on the outturn. If these start going off course, it is important for the management to be aware of it quickly and to know how to react. It is best able to do this if possible divergences from the plan have been considered beforehand and if contingency plans have been prepared to deal with them. Contingency plans may be prepared for a number of key pressure points, for instance:

— order intake and mix
— gross margins
— fixed cost base
— liquidity.

It is important for managers to evaluate the consequences of what may happen if some of the assumptions affecting key elements of the plan turn out to be invalid. Quite small changes in certain factors can have disproportionate consequences.

The technique of measuring the consequences is known as 'sensitivity analysis'. Because a large number of possibilities may have to be considered, the use of a computer will be most helpful.

It is in relation to such sensitive factors that contingency plans will have special application.

Summary

Appendix 5 is a summary of the principal elements considered in this chapter.

Appendix 6 is an actual business plan prepared by a company which had only commenced business some three years prior to its preparation. The same style of plan had been used from the beginning.

Although each year there were some material variations from plan (some for exceptional reasons), the broad thrust of the business development did follow the intended pattern. The sale of the company took place some two years later (earlier than had originally been contemplated) with actual results for that year right on plan, and with anticipated growth significantly ahead of plan for the ensuing year.

This particular company had been financed by a merchant bank which had made available all the loan monies in consideration for 20 per cent of the equity. From the commencement, the board consisted of an equal number of executive and non-executive directors, contributing a variety of skills and experience which were substantially responsible for the company's success.

Case study

The following case study draws together some of the points discussed in this chapter, and provides a chance to consider them in relation to a practical situation.

A well established family business, 'A', had been trading profitably for many years. It perceived the future of its class of business threatened, and decided to commence operations in business 'B' as a defensive move. Within three years the whole picture had changed. Heavy investment and operating losses in business 'B' were threatening the total business, and the company bankers who had not taken a negative attitude were strongly pressing for a plan of action which would reassure them that the business would survive and the loans be repaid on schedule. The action taken followed the course set out below.

Step 1

A rapid and relatively simple investigation took place, in cooperation with a consultant who had practical experience in the business. Within approximately one week the investigation disclosed that the company/management accounts were prepared regularly, but did not readily reveal what was happening in the respective businesses.

The request was made for there to be produced within three days a breakdown of the business into its discrete parts 'A' and 'B' for the preceding four years, disclosing for each: turnover; gross margin; margin percentage; variable costs; contribution; fixed costs; net margin; margin percentage. This did not present a difficult problem. The information was available, but had not previously been presented in a useful way.

The figures immediately disclosed the rapidly deteriorating situation in business 'B'. A solution was required within weeks.

Step 2

A projection was prepared of the results for the next three years, including the results of an intended acquisition to enhance the strength of business 'A', to be funded by further borrowings. Estimated balance sheets were prepared for end years 1, 2 and 3.

Step 3

Taking business 'B', it was immediately evident that, with the contribution margins being achieved, and with the fixed overheads, the required break-even turnover was at least two and a half times existing turnover.

The conclusion was that either the business should be sold or trading should be discontinued forthwith.

It was further concluded that there was no prospect of a realistic sale of business 'B' as a going concern. Therefore the business should be closed.

Step 4

The costs of closure of business 'B' were estimated, including redundancy pay, stock losses, debt collections, losses on plant (some on lease) and on factory closure. The cash element of the closure costs and of any ongoing costs on a mothball basis were calculated.

Step 5
The balance sheet, projected to the current year end, was reviewed. After writing off acquisition goodwill and costs of closing business 'B' (wherever they might actually be charged in the accounts) there would be a deficit, though probably a manageable one.

Step 6
A tourniquet having been applied to the cash bleeding, the next step was to start strengthening the cash position of the company by:

- disposing of those assets not actively employed in the business (which included three properties)
- reviewing current assets and liabilities with the objective of releasing some of the cash tied up in the net current assets.

Step 7
It was considered that these steps would lead to a positive cash flow, but that even allowing for a free tax holiday arising from trading losses (the necessary safeguards had been taken to protect them from tax), all available operational cash resources would be needed for a period of around five years in order to run down the current borrowings.

Step 8
During the next six months, a business plan covering the ensuing three years was prepared. It was clear that no formal business plan had previously been prepared for either business 'A' or business 'B'. To have engaged in new business without careful planning was commercially very risky. Although business 'A' and business 'B' might have looked similar, a proper market study before entry would have revealed business 'B' to be in a totally different business from that of 'A'.

The brief for the preparation of the business plan included the following points:

- Do not at this time pre-empt any possible options.
- Keep in mind the possible need to re-enter business 'B', but on a totally different basis and under properly controlled conditions. A totally separate management structure to be responsible for that business (with potential for overall control of the business) was envisaged.
- Examine the principal trading locations and consider whether location X should be disposed of, or whether the whole business could be relocated to X, releasing location Y for sale.
- Present alternative proposals if necessary.
- Consider the financial implications and the possibility of introducing a new equity investor and the basis of such investment.

The crucial management factors which this case highlights are:

- Understanding and defining the business in which a company is operating (see p63)

- preparing a carefully structured business plan, which is of greatest importance when it is intended to open up a new business
- definition by the board of the management information it must receive in order properly to control the business (see p63-4)
- clarifying management responsibility for different business activities.

Chapter 5

Control Through the Budget

The budget is often thought of as an accounting exercise. This is totally wrong. The budget is the financial reflection of the annual plan and both documents are the responsibility of management.

The annual plan

We have discussed how a business plan should cover a period of three to five years. The first year, however, needs to be dealt with separately and in much greater detail in what is usually referred to as the annual plan. It is the annual plan which provides the basic financial information from which the budget is produced.

The structure of the annual plan is similar to that used in the longer range plan, but it is more specific, in much greater detail, and concentrates on tactics rather than overall strategy. The thoroughness with which a plan is prepared is often an indication of its credibility.

For example, the manpower section might address itself to the following (where appropriate, broken down by period):

- general personnel policies
- staff numbers, by category
- retirements during the year
- expected losses
- recruitment plans
- management resources and plans
- development programmes
- training programmes
- employee communication and involvement
- employee shareholdings/options
- employee remuneration plans
- pensions/insurance plans
- financial implications
- administrative changes (eg computerisation of records).

The fulfilment of the objectives set out in the annual plan and budget depends largely on the commitment to them of individual managers. The managing director should therefore discuss the objectives with his subordinate managers and make sure there is a complete understanding of what each of them is expected to achieve. Each manager must then go through a similar process with his own subordinates.

The procedures for monitoring progress must be agreed and set down in the annual plan.

Budget format

The financial expression of the plan might be presented as a budget along the following lines:

1. Key assumptions
2. Summary of the budget, including key ratios
3. Forecast profit and loss account, by period
4. Forecast balance sheet at end (intermediate balance sheets will also be required)
5. Forecast source and application of funds
6. Forecast cash flows, by period
7. Notes to the budget
8. Illustrative visual material, such as graphs, bar charts, etc as may be thought helpful.

The development of detailed action plans to improve the chances of achieving the annual plan will be found most helpful to the board of the company, to the managing director, and to those with the detailed responsibility for parts of the plan.

Appendix 7 illustrates the manner in which an action plan might be developed, in effect bringing together in summary form the key elements of the annual plan.

Progress should be formally reviewed at least quarterly. It will be useful to put the budget in context by supplying figures for the two preceding years and the expected results for the current year (remember that the budget is likely to be prepared some time before the end of the current year).

The budget is drawn up in relation to the natural activities of the business, and areas of income and expenditure are clearly shown so that levels of performance and causes of variance from plan can be easily identified. Whenever possible, it is important that profit or cost centres recorded in the budget should relate directly to the responsibilities of individual managers.

The budget is prepared to coincide with the company financial year. It must therefore be in place before that year starts, although the nearer the commencement date the more accurate forecasts are likely to be. In large operations the budget requires considerable staff and accounting work, and adequate time must be allowed for the necessary analysis work to be done, for outline plans to be prepared, discussed and amended, and for the final document to be drafted and submitted to the board for approval. The management team responsible for preparation of the budget often support it with a presentation and discussion. This should ensure a thorough understanding of the implications of the plan, and commitment by the board and the senior executive team to its achievement.

The budget is a key control mechanism, so it is not satisfactory to fix it for a whole year; it is necessary to be able to make checks and changes from time to time. It must therefore be built up in shorter periods — most naturally on a monthly basis. Some businesses operate on the basis of 13 four-weekly periods, but the majority adopt a 4-, 4-, 5-week basis to permit quarterly and half-yearly reconciliations. Either method allows for proper reflection of seasonal influences. Consistency is clearly desirable, with as few changes as possible being made to the frequency and composition of the budget. This helps managers to understand and implement it. It also facilitates comparison with preceding years or periods.

Sales plan and budget

Preliminary work

The overall market analysis and strategy will have been established in the longer term business plan. The annual plan and budget must be concerned with the detail of methods and costs.

In reaching decisions on some of these matters and in developing plans there may be a need to use market research, an advertising agency and public relations advisers.

Discussions will be necessary between sales and production management about the planned sales volumes, factory capacity, unit costs and many other related problems.

Stock policies must be determined by the board. How much of each raw material should be held, bearing in mind delivery lead times, sources of supply, factory efficiency and stocking facilities? How much finished goods stock must be held to allow for efficient production runs and to meet customer requirements in markets which usually refuse to conform to planned levels?

Stocks can be a substantial investment, almost certainly related to sales volumes, with a significant bearing on working capital requirements (and therefore on financing costs) and must be considered in relation to warehousing facilities, distribution methods and stock turnover rates. The actual mix and levels of stock held need constant monitoring.

The sales manager therefore needs much detailed information to prepare his sales plan which, in a business of any complexity, will be contained in a separate document.

The sales plan

For each product and sector, the sales plan will embrace:

— order intake, backlog, unit volumes, sales revenues, gross margins
— the method of achieving sales:
  ● Direct representation, wholesale, agency, direct mail, or a combination of two or more of these
— the organisation of the sales force, including the number and timing of sales people needed, their skills and locations
— the allocation of sales quotas to each person responsible for sales
— sales commissions and other incentives
— nature and cost of support to be given to each sector, including advertising, promotional literature, catalogues and other aids
— promotional and discount offers, when and to whom
— distribution channels for delivery of product to the customer:
  ● Road, rail or air; own fleet; contract fleet
— stock locations and levels, minimum drops
— exhibitions and trade fairs
— demonstrations and presentations
— training of sales people and possibly customers also
— after-sales servicing arrangements
— sales budget reflecting the above elements, including all sales costs for which the sales manager will be held responsible
— reporting and communication requirements

For the purposes of the budget, only the summarised results will be necessary and in simplified form may be presented for each product as in the example shown in Figure 5.1.

Month	1	2	3	4	5	etc
Order intake						
Volume	300	200	400	600	400	
Value £	1500	1000	2000	3300	2200	
Sales £	1750	1500	1000	2000	3300	
Promotion costs	—	—	—	200	250	
Advertising costs	—	250	350	—	—	
Gross margin	25%	25%	25%	30%	30%	

Figure 5.1. *Summary of budget for each product*

In this example, the sales figures for the first month are derived from orders in month 12 of the preceding year; it is assumed that despatch and invoicing follow one month after order. If it is planned to increase order cover to, say, three months, the order intake will need to be larger during the build-up period (or billings will be lower). The totals of the various product lines provide the monthly revenues, margins and sales costs for the sales budget. This presentation provides an opportunity for the board to check whether the targets set for gross margin on each product are being met.

The same information is likely to be required to be presented in different ways. For example, sales volumes planned through different distribution channels might be set out as in Figure 5.2.

	Last year				Budget						Total year	
£	%	Gross margin %	Sales outlet	Q1	Q2	Q3	Q4	£	%	Gross margin %
			Multiple (eg stores, DIY centres, etc)							
			Wholesale							
			Mail order							
			Export							
	100							100		

Figure 5.2. *Sales volume shown according to distribution channel*

Manufacturing plan and budget

These will be developed in parallel with the sales plan and budget. If planned margins are to be achieved, the establishment of costs is essential, whether products are bought in or manufactured. Manufacturing costs are especially difficult to forecast. They depend, among other things, on the costs of raw materials (exchange risks may be an additional problem here), labour rates, productivity, reject rates, quality control and factory work loading.

There is likely to be a great deal of discussion before the optimum levels of production and planned sales are arrived at. Practical factory loading may be the most important factor, and this may be seen to be about 80 per cent of potential working single shift; standard costs are then based on this assumed level of activity. Fixed overheads are 'recovered' in the product costs by spreading them more or less equitably between the units of production. Reality is most unlikely to conform with the plan. It is therefore necessary for management to be able quickly to compare actual performance with budget and establish the source or sources of variance at the end of each accounting period. Work measurement is often necessary to determine reasonable productivity standards.

The aim of the manufacturing budget is thus to establish the cost of goods required to support the sales plan. As with the sales plan, each product or product group must be isolated to establish the margins applicable to each. Satisfactory product margins are vital in determining pricing policies; as well as setting the margins to be achieved, the board should also set minimum margins below which, except under controlled conditions, the products will not be sold. Cost of goods sold is only one factor to be kept under review in relation to pricing – the essential factor is the ability to meet market conditions on a profitable basis.

Overhead costs

The next stage of the budget concerns the other costs incurred in conducting the business. Each needs to be considered on its merits, and in the light of general business policies. In an expanding business, it is almost always necessary to plan changes in the organisation before the increased revenues are actually received; This applies particularly to marketing and selling costs. It must be ensured that the overheads do not become insupportable if the anticipated revenue does not materialise. The proportion of revenue to be allocated to each category of overhead will have been dealt with in the long-term business plan, and the budget must be broadly in line with this ratio.

The budget is easier to understand if the overheads are grouped into related items of expenditure, with the group totals being shown in the principal income and expenditure statement, and the precise composition of each group shown in supporting schedules.

The grouping might be:

- marketing and sales expenses
- general overhead expenses
- financial expenses
- research and development expenses

The budget is a complete set of financial plans against which actual results can be compared as they emerge, period by period. It also provides a means of ready comparison with the previous year; most managements are reluctant to forget the previous year's performance, even though the really vital comparison is with the plan.

Profit reprojections

All budgets need to be reviewed from time to time, and new projections made in the light of the current situation. If events have departed significantly from plan, it is fairly useless for management to continue comparing actual performance period by period with a budget prepared some time previously — it can be almost a year in the last quarter of the budget year. A budget which has ceased to be relevant tends to be disregarded by managers. Reviews may take place at six-monthly intervals, but a formal review at quarterly intervals is by far the better way. As the current environment is assessed, results can be reprojected period by period to the year end, built on the actual results achieved at the date of the projection. These projections should be clearly numbered and dated and may be conveniently referred to as P1, P2, etc to distinguish them from the budget.

It should not be understood from this that the budget is abandoned. It never should be. It is the anchor for the financial year. Measuring actual results against the latest projection for the period makes it easier to decide on the appropriate actions to take, but cumulative results should be compared with both the budget and the latest projection. It is important to know the cumulative deviations from the original plan.

Reprojected cash flows and balance sheets must also be prepared to provide a continuous, sound control mechanism. A good management accountant can produce revised outline projections on a monthly basis if required.

How all this comes together will be demonstrated in Chapter 7.

Management targets

A budget which has been realistically prepared, preferably on the conservative side, allows the board to motivate management to achieve higher targets. The substantial contingency item in Appendix 6 was intended to reflect the potential for the year, and management were encouraged to go for the higher results which the board felt reasonably attainable.

The profit achieved in excess of budget can provide bonuses for the management and other employees. It could be agreed, for instance, that 20 per cent of the profit in excess of budget should be the bonus potential. Actual performance is then compared each month and cumulatively with target performance, as well as with budget, by adjustment to the contingency provision.

Capital expenditure budget

This budget shows in detail the capital expenditure needed to achieve the operating budget (or to anticipate the requirements of a subsequent year). Although this expenditure is approved in principle at the time the budget is adopted, all significant items of expenditure (definition of which depends on the size and nature of the business) should be specifically approved by the board before final commitment of funds. Approval should not normally be given without a financial justification for the expenditure having been prepared.

Balance sheet

Forecast balanace sheets are prepared from the operating budget, the capital budget, and certain assumptions which must be agreed with management. They may relate only to the position at the end of the budget financial year, but are more likely also to show the forecast position at each quarter end or month end. In this way planned changes in assets and liabilities can be indicated, particularly as they affect working capital, so that the consequences can be considered well before they materialise.

Cash flow

Cash flow forecasts are similarly based on the operating and capital budgets, and the assumptions used for the forecast balance sheets. They are prepared by period to coincide with the operating statements. Cash management is the subject of the next chapter.

Chapter 6

Cash Management

Unless the wages can be paid on Friday, every Friday, there will soon be no more Fridays on which to continue in business (Genghis Khan Guide to Business).

The management of cash is absolutely crucial to the control of a business. The very survival of a business may be put in jeopardy by failing to manage the cash flow in a tight situation. The recession of the 1970s has brought about a strong appreciation of this fact among UK companies.

An example of the importance of strong cash control in a crisis is provided by the Rank Organisation. Many years ago, in spite of a complicated operational structure and in the order of 40-50,000 on the payroll, for a period no discretion could be accorded to subordinate managements, particularly where very substantial sums were involved in the making of motion pictures. The group managing director therefore assumed direct control of cash within the organisation and each week subsidiary company requisitions were submitted to the group, summarised and aggregated, then reviewed by the managing director who authorised cash releases. By this method the situation was controlled and, in due course, stabilised. Not surprisingly, for years thereafter strong central cash control was a feature of the group's procedures. In this, as in a number of areas, Rank was many years ahead of its time.

Another example is provided by a European property development company which had got into serious cash difficulties caused by the same factors experienced by UK property developers in the mid-seventies. It had a speculative property portfolio, probably 60 per cent unlet, spread through three European countries, with very significant total borrowings in several unmatched currencies. It had no choice but to meet its liabilities, because the borrowings were guaranteed by a UK sterling source. Properties which were unlet and, in some cases, incomplete, rapidly rising interest rates and a falling pound looked like a recipe for a financial disaster. The solution lay in putting rigid controls on expenditure and making the generation of cash flow management's most urgent task.

Liquidity in business is the acid test. If commitments cannot be met as they fall due in the normal course, the business is illiquid and it will cease to operate. Cash management is therefore the single most important factor in business operation. Direct responsibility for cash management in a large company lies with the treasurer; in smaller companies it lies with the finance director or accountant. In all cases the managing director must make it a prime concern of his own.

To control cash effectively, all the underlying causes of cash movements have to be considered. The management of cash is therefore all about the management of the balance sheet.

Profit and cash

Profit and cash are, of course, related — but they are not the same (except, perhaps, in the rather basic case of a business which deals only in cash). They are not the same because, for example, businesses work on credit, have stocks to carry and assets to finance.

A business can be profitable without being liquid, or liquid without being profitable. Both profit and liquidity are essential to a successful ongoing business. Short-term liquidity difficulties can, and do, cause profitable businesses to fail.

Profit is the surplus remaining after charging against income all the costs incurred in earning that income. Some of those costs are not cash-related, in the short term, such as the charge for depreciation, which writes off the cost of a fixed asset over its estimated useful life. Cash flow statements forecast the in-flows and out-flows of cash, and the timing and extent of resultant surplus or deficit. Deficits have to be corrected either by attempting to adjust the timing of some of the cash movements, or by borrowing in one form or another, or by raising additional shareholders' capital. Movements of cash are of great importance to the continuity of the business, in the short term, but profit is the basis of long-term survival and growth: retained profit is a primary source of capital for development. If there are borrowings, interest must be paid and the level of borrowings kept within limits and rules agreed with the lender.

Cash forecasts

It is convenient to consider the preparation of cash forecasts under three headings:

- long-range forecasts
- annual (budget) forecasts
- short-range forecasts.

Long-range forecasts

As discussed in Chapter 4, plans for a period of three to five years should be set out in a business plan. Although actual results rarely coincide with those forecast, the plan provides a necessary framework within which to work. Preparation of the plan is of considerable value in itself, and the objectives established therein should remain in sight, whatever unplanned developments take place.

It is worth while preparing cash flows and profit forecasts on a quarterly basis for the first year or two, and thereafter on an annual basis. There are almost bound to be considerable variations in cash flow during the course of a year, but for long-range purposes, this is not very important. Profit forecasts, cash flows and year-end target balance sheets are all interrelated. Together with capital expenditure plans, these financial models draw attention to significant danger requiring some variation or redrawing of the plans; they also provide an opportunity to consider and explore appropriate funding sources.

An example of the value of long-range planning is provided by a computer based company. The growth anticipated in the company's five-year plans was ambitious (as, in a field of rapid technological development, it probably should be). The plan was to develop two new related but different businesses financed by funds generated by the original business together with substantial bank and shareholder finance. The financial models demonstrated that the feasibility of the project depended on a few specific events going more or less according to plan, especially in the first three years. The board was able to identify the events which would involve the greatest degree of risk and agree with management key points at which the situation would be reviewed, and further financial commitment would be made only after a positive decision. Of course, this approach does not remove all risk, but reassessing potential risks at periodic intervals allows time for a change of plan, or the slowing down of developments as circumstances dictate.

Long-range planning is sometimes rejected as of little practical value. But in addition to the benefits which the computer company above recognised, the considerable involvement which the preparation of the plans requires of managers usually turns out to be very worthwhile in itself.

It is argued that forecasts for three to five years ahead are likely to be so inaccurate that it is wasteful of executive time to attempt this kind of planning. But it is a fact that certain matters, such as the acquisition of additional premises, the development of international business or the research and development of new products cannot be properly assessed except within such a framework.

Annual forecast
Chapter 5 referred to the need to prepare a cash forecast for the year in parallel with, and as part of, the annual plan and budget.

This cannot usefully be done with the broad brush adopted for the long-term framework. Many factors affect the movement of cash, some of which can be very significant at different points in the year: for example, receipts and payments on capital account; the need to lay out substantial forward funds, such as in some areas of the holiday trade; the seasonality of the retail trade, or as in a publishing business dependent for most of its income on advertising revenues.

The annual cash forecast is, therefore, drawn up either by quarterly or, preferably, by monthly periods to coincide with the profit budgets. It must cover each item of income and expense as it is likely to occur, although with experience some short-cutting is possible. The data required for the forecast balance sheets are also required for the preparation of the cash flows.

Forecasts of sales revenues need to take account of credit periods. 'Payment at the end of the month following that in which goods are invoiced' may be asked for, and this implies an average period of credit of six weeks. It is most unlikely that all debts will be paid on due date. It is necessary to anticipate what may happen in practice; experience might show, for instance, that payments for UK sales are received as follows:

on due date	70%
within the next month	25%
and in the next following month	5%
	100%

Some provision might have to be built in for bad debts: a consumer credit business, for example, may well assume in its planning that 2½ per cent of all advances will not be repaid.

The pattern for overseas sales may well include longer periods of credit. Greater care is needed in tracking payments outside the UK, and currency translation may be one of many additional problems. The cash flow forecast is constructed along the lines set out in Figure 6.1.

Cash flow forecast for the period ending . . . .

Period	1	2	3	*	*	*	12	Total for year (£)
Receipts								
Debtors								
VAT								
Other								
A: Total receipts								
Payments								
Creditors								
Employment								
Rent								
VAT								
etc								
B: Total payments								
Cash operating surplus/deficit (A−B)								
Interest payable								
Capital expenditure								
Net surplus/deficit for period								
Add cash balance (overdraft) at beginning of period								
Cash balance (overdraft) at end of period								

Figure 6.1. *Format for cash flow forecast*

Short-range forecasts

These are best prepared for the three months ahead, month by month. They follow the general format of the cash flow forecast above, and are rolled forward at the end of each month. In a tight cash situation, the cash forecast for the month immediately ahead may be prepared on a weekly basis, and a manager may decide that to retain control of the business when the company is very close to its approved overdraft limits, all expenditure needs to be specifically authorised. The continuing supply of raw materials must be ensured, whereas some payments can if necessary be deferred on a short-term basis. An example of a rolling cash forecast in shown in Appendix 8.

An example of a short-term cash forecast submitted by an accountant to his managing director for approval is shown in Appendix 9.

Each month, actual cash movements should be compared with the plan for the corresponding period, and the causes of significant variations summarised by the accountant for the managing director.

Source and application of funds

This matter was dealt with above (p52). It is a statement which needs to be prepared at the end of each reporting period as part of the management accounts package. It provides an explanation of cash inflows and outflows and, most importantly, identifies their implications for working capital.

It is useful to include in the statement:

- the position in the preceding reporting period
- the plan (or forecast) for the period under consideration
- the cumulative situation since the commencement of the financial year.

Management of working capital

The management of working capital is an integral part of the management of cash. The term 'working capital' applies to those assets and liabilities which are 'current' or 'quick' — constantly turning over on a short-term basis. The principal components in a trading company will be:

Assets	stock
	debtors
	prepayments
Liabilities	trade creditors
	expense accruals.

There will also be cash at bank, or an overdraft. The difference between current assets and liabilities will be shown as 'net current assets'.

The composition varies greatly according to the nature of the business. In some cases, there are significant customer deposits or payments on account. An insurance company usually works with substantial bank balances, because premiums are payable in advance whereas claims arise over a period of time. Working credit balances can often be put to good use, but this should be done with caution. There was a case once of an insurance company which had ceased trading but valid claims were still arising many years later, in US dollars against a depreciating sterling (in which the company operated); it was impossible to estimate the cash resources required to meet the run-off of liabilities.

Included within the working capital requirements should be those amounts payable on longer-term obligations but falling due within the next 12 months. These may occur under hire purchase agreements, or where a medium-term loan is being repaid by regular instalments. It is useful to look in close detail at the make-up of working capital.

Trade debtors

A sale is effected only when cash has been collected. Granting credit to customers has to be done with circumspection. You need to have adequate means of funding the build-up of trade debtors, and you must be as sure as possible that the debt will in fact be collected on the due date. Granting credit is a cost to the vendor in terms of interest for the period the debt is outstanding, administration of procedures and bookkeeping and, possibly, legal costs. It is not of much practical value to know you have a sound legal case against the debtor, because the costs and time involved mean working capital locked up and a potential bad debt to write off.

Credit control policy

A company credit control policy must be established by the board and adhered to. There are potential internal conflicts of interest between the sales manager and the accountant. The credit rating of each customer must be known (several avenues of enquiry can be followed up) and each customer must be given a credit limit.

Trading terms must be determined: the normal period of credit; deposits with order basis of price quotation, and so on. Disputes can arise when terms of the seller and purchaser differ in their respective documentation: the greatest care needs to be exercised to avoid disputes.

Cash discounts of 2½ or 5 per cent are often offered in order to secure early payment. This is quite expensive. Assuming the gain is a 30-day reduction in credit, the cost is effectively either 30 or 60 per cent respectively a year.

Bad debts are very costly to a business. Effective procedures to secure payments must be activated as soon as the credit period expires; involving a debt collection or similar agency at an early stage often produces good results. Sales departments often object to this course of action, but a look at the costs shows how necessary it is: if the net trading margin is 10 per cent, a bad debt of £1,000 is equivalent to eliminating profit on sales of £10,000. In the case of a bank, which may be working on a ½ per cent turn, the damaging consequences of a bad debt are obvious.

Administration of debts

The prompt issue of invoices is very important. Payment terms may be, for example, 30 days after invoice or the end of the month following that in which the invoice is issued. Either way, the date of invoice issue is important, and in some cases can save 30 days' credit. For example, a publisher issuing invoices to advertisers on the last day of the month may take considerable trouble getting an advance copy of the advertisement to submit with the invoice.

Analyse the debtors at the end of each month, showing the extent to which uncollected debts have aged. An increasing percentage of overdue debts is an indication of the need for more effective action.

Export sales require special vigilance. Thorough credit enquiries must be made and it is often wise to arrange insurance cover through ECGD. Insurance cover for UK debtors may be considered but it is not always available.

The management accounts must show the average days credit outstanding. This should be compared with company policy standard and disclose the trend. The formula for calculating the ratio is:

$$\frac{\text{debtors outstanding}}{\text{average days sales}} = \text{average days credit}$$

eg: $\dfrac{£150,000 \ \times \ 30 \text{ days}}{£100,000} = 45 \text{ days}$
(sales per month)

Stocks

These may comprise:

- raw materials
- finished stocks
- work in progress
- miscellaneous (eg stationery, etc).

Spare parts and service parts may also involve substantial sums, but require separate consideration.

The management of stock in trade is critical and should be the subject of board policy. Each type of stock needs to be looked at separately.

Raw materials are a production requirement. The levels are affected by the production process and rate of factory turnover. Average unit production time might be one day or it might be one month. The lead delivery time varies too. Materials coming from abroad may differ from a local source of supply. Consideration must be given to the possibility of delivery disruption and of alternative supply sources. Irregularity of production plays havoc with stock levels.

The policy must establish the minimum and maximum stock levels (by principal component), the order lead time and the minimum order amount.

In the case of finished goods, the primary consideration is the servicing of customers. Factors include the minimum order drop, the method of delivery, the extent to which sales fluctuate and how quickly delivery is necessary to meet customer requirements and remain competitive.

Management accounts must show:

$$\frac{\text{cost of goods sold}}{\text{average stock level}} \quad = \quad \text{month's supply of stock}$$

This calculation is best based on the *forward* estimate (say, for the next three months) of cost of goods sold, as this is most relevant to the stock situation.

The rate of stock turnover is critical to every business in which stock is carried. For example, if stocks are valued at £250,000 and turnover is £1m per annum, stocks are turning on average four times. If this can be increased to five turns (without adverse trading consequences), the average stock level can be reduced to £200,000, a saving of £50,000. As stock carrying can well cost 20 per cent or more, this means an annual profit improvement of £10,000. If the target pre-tax profit return is 10 per cent, that is £100,000 per annum, the stock reduction is equivalent to 10 per cent of the annual profit.

Stock obsolescence must also be mentioned. The physical stock lists should be carefully scrutinised at least annually, possibly quarterly.

Proper management of stocks implies accurate records being kept of goods moving into factory stock, into production and into finished goods. As soon as practicable, these records need to be put on to the computer, but this must be recognised as a tricky operation requiring most careful management.

Finally, do not overlook stocks 'on loan' to customers. Sales results may be improved if products can be got on to customer premises, even if not formally contracted. On the other hand, the practice needs very careful control.

Trade creditors

The reverse side of the coin is the management of trade creditors. Again regular monthly information is necessary with regard to the ageing of creditors and average days credit taken.

In seeking the maximum credit period, which will reduce working capital requirements, care must be taken not to go too far. Your creditors are putting precisely the same checks on you as you are putting on your debtors. Regularity of settlement is frequently of greater comfort to the supplier than the actual period of credit. Pushed too far, a supplier will cut off supplies and this can be a very expensive matter. A weak relationship with suppliers militates against a smooth running business operation and good purchasing policies: this again means additional cost.

The existence of creditors means that commitments have already been made. Firm policies must be established concerning the authority to enter into orders or commitments and the limits of that authority. In certain cases the authority to commit funds should be retained by the board, such as when material amounts are involved or when there are long-term implications for the company. It must be remembered that internal limits on authority to enter a commitment are of no concern to the supplier, and cannot be used as grounds for opting out of a commitment.

Net operating assets

More attention is generally paid to the profit and loss account than to the balance sheet, but most managers do recognise the crucial importance of cash management which can only be achieved by control of the assets and liabilities which comprise the balance sheet.

The relevance of working capital to that process was discussed above (p99). For some purposes, however, the management of net operating assets (which include working capital) can also be valuable. 'Net operating assets' (NOA) are all those assets and liabilities which enable the business to function, excluding cash balances and/or bank overdrafts.

The rate of turnover of NOA is a key indicator in asset management. The ratio is:

$$\frac{\text{sales revenues}}{\text{NOA}} = \text{turn rates}$$

The board should establish its requirements of management by setting the target rate of turnover. The faster the rate of turnover, the less capital will be used in the business and the greater the relative profitability. If, for example, revenues are £1m a year and NOA amount to £250,000, they are being turned on average four times a year.

Net profit margin is the amount remaining after charging against revenue all costs incurred in its earning. The ratio is:

$$\frac{\text{net profit}}{\text{sales revenues}} \times 100 = \text{net margin \%}$$

As with NOA, net margin will vary significantly from one business to another, perhaps 3 per cent or less in the food business to 15 per cent or over in a well run technology company. The higher the margin, the better – provided that the search for high margins does not adversely affect sales and produce an absolute reduction in profits.

If the two factors are now brought together, then:

NOA turn x net margin %   =   return on operating capital

So, for example:

4 x 10%   =   40% on operating capital

The extent to which the rate of turn of NOA and/or the net margins can be increased is directly reflected in improved overall profitability of the business. An asset turn of five, instead of four, will raise return on employed assets from 40 to 50 per cent. The board must, therefore, as part of its financial objectives, establish the required rate of turn of NOA, and the net margin on sales revenues.

Funding working capital

The vital importance of the working capital requirement is often not sufficiently appreciated by management, or even sometimes by accountants. Cash strain in a rapidly expanding business is very great and a constant threat to survival. As discussed in Chapter 3, most companies have to fund part of their working capital requirements from their own (shareholder) resources.

The relationship between working capital requirements and turnover is likely to be stable but, as illustrated in Chapter 3, different depending upon the nature of the business. If only 50 per cent of the working capital requirement is provided by the bank, the other half has to be found from internal resources. Therefore, the business must earn sufficient profit to be able to do that.

In the UK, bank overdraft finance is the normal and most sensible method of financing working capital because of the short-term and fluctuating levels which may be involved. Net profit margins must therefore be adequate to take the strain of bank interest — probably 3 per cent over base rate; and another 3 per cent if the government guarantee scheme is available for a new business start-up.

Summary

The management of cash is a very important aspect of operating any business, large or small. The managing director must be involved. The importance of strict central control of cash, particularly in industry and commerce, has been receiving much more attention recently in the UK. With substantial cash flows, the earnings of quite small improved margins and the correct anticipation of application dates can make important contributions to profit without any additional capital resources. The management of assets is a key requirement in the cash management process.

Chapter 7

Monitoring Performance

There are many reasons why companies fail. What is to be regretted is that, all too often, it is due to lack of effective monitoring — either by the company or the bank. The directors, for instance, may feel it an expensive luxury to pay for their accountants to prepare monthly figures — and they do not have the necessary competence 'in house'...
(Accountancy, *February 1985*)

It is essential for the board to monitor all aspects of the business which bear on operating performance. The board should be kept informed on a monthly basis — in practice perhaps 10 times a year — at the earliest reasonable date in the month when management accounts can be produced, reported on by management and considered — this should be during the second or third week of the month.

At the end of each quarter, there should be a more formal review of the results and, as has been indicated previously, a reprojection of the forecast annual results.

The board should indicate precisely what reports it requires and the frequency with which it wishes to receive them. There is a military adage: 'Time spent on reconnaissance is seldom wasted'. Like a military organisation, a business is heavily dependent on information to make timely and well judged decisions. At the same time, of course, the collection and assembly of precise information must not take so long that it is completed too late to be of value in decision making. With good planning, key information can be made available quickly and at reasonable cost.

Information is of two types: that gathered externally about the market-place and the activities of competitors; and that generated internally about the conduct of the business and its performance. Appendix 10 indicates the type of routine reports which may be required.

Information requirements

Management should aim to provide the essential information in the simplest, most easily assimilated form possible, using a minimum of technical language. It is often helpful to have the figures supplemented by a visual presentation in chart or graph form.

The board needs not only factual information: it also needs interpretation. This should be provided by simple notes with the figures, and a brief written report by the managing director issued in time to give all board members an opportunity to reflect on the contents before the meeting. Reports and figures should be in the hands of the directors at least three days, and preferably up to seven days, before the meeting. So the monthly timetable leading up to the next meeting might be:

105

day 1 or 2   sales figures
day 10   management accounts available to management
day 13   accounts and MD report issued to board
day 20   board meeting
day 23   issue minutes

Format of financial reports

The reporting system should include the following:

Schedule 1. Summary of operating results, key ratios and key information
Schedule 2. Profit and loss account (with supporting schedules as necessary)
Schedule 3. Order intake and sales analysis
Schedule 4. Balance sheet
Schedule 5. Source and application of funds.

It is good practice to include here, as a matter of routine, information about any legal actions in which the company may be involved. The board then has a chance to consider how they should be handled, before there is heavy commitment.

In respect of each schedule, the following should be shown:

— the actual results for the period
— the cumulative results for the period to date.

These results need to be compared with:

— the plan (budget)
— the previous year

and, when a reprojection of the results has taken place, the comparisons will be varied as follows:

— for the period, with the reprojected result for that period (in replacement of the budget)
— cumulatively, with both the budget and with the reprojected results.

To complete the picture, it is necessary to show:

— the planned results for the year
— the reprojected results for the year
— the actual results for the preceding year.

Orders

The order position is a key indicator of future sales. It is important to know:

— the opening order backlog
— orders received in the period
— orders converted to sales in the period
— the closing backlog.

Volumes and values are important statistics, but the profit content of orders taken must also be shown. The gross margin contained in the order intake and backlog reveals whether or not expectations are going to be realised, and there may be time for action to be taken if necessary.

The order state covers the same principal products as the sales analysis.

Break-even

Included in the summary of results should be the sales break-even figure required to meet the projected expense run rate for the three months immediately ahead. This can be compared with the budget (or reprojected) sales plans for the corresponding period, so that again there is advance notice of likely results, which is what really matters to management.

Provided the reporting systems follow a format similar to that suggested, there should normally be no need to spend a great deal of time reviewing past results, and more time is available to consider proposed action plans and development of the business.

Purposes of a monitoring system

The principal purposes of a monitoring system are:

— to know currently where the business is
— to know how that compares with where it was intended to be
— to identify the causes of variation and to determine action plans
— to consider on a regular basis management performance against objectives
— to encourage regular communication throughout the business through review of results and achievements
— to forecast on a regular basis the estimated annual results and the consequent implications.

The greatest importance should be attached to the correlation between operating results and personal performance, between the setting of objectives and the review of achievement.

Appendix 11 shows different ways in which financial information may be reported. They are capable of infinite adaptation, and management must find the most appropriate form for the company according to what information is of greatest importance to business progress and how that information is to be responded to. It may be necessary from time to time to add reports on particular aspects of the business. It is important in such cases to stop producing the data as soon as it has served its purpose. It is worthwhile making sure that the routine reports and information systems are reviewed periodically. There is a common tendency to keep reports running long after they have ceased to be of value. The rule is: concentrate on that which is relevant; scrap that which is not.

Value added statements

Value added is the key element in business effectiveness. It represents the increase in value of a product or service as a result of the work done to it in any particular business. The importance of the concept seems to be insufficiently appreciated. The practice of preparing value added statements is therefore relatively unusual, but well worthwhile.

They can be most valuable in explaining to employees (and the board) the wealth creating process within the company. The statement identifies the contributions made by employees, shareholders and finance. It can play a part in a bonus system for employees.

An example of a value added statement is given in Appendix 12.

The value added concept can also be of considerable help in tracking down the sources of profitability. Profit can only be generated if value added per hour of labour exceeds costs per hour. To be of value to management each product, service or contract will need to be separately analysed for value added and attributable labour time and cost.

The management object must be to widen the gap between hourly value added and cost. This can only be done by identifying and considering separately each element entering into the make-up of the calculation.

The application of the value added concept may be particularly useful to service and financial businesses. In one case the concept was successfully applied in a service business, to the considerable benefit of the company and its employees.

Capital expenditure audits

In many companies it is the practice for recommendations to incur capital expenditure to be made by management to the board, and approved. The board should ensure that the actual results of that investment are periodically compared with the original submission to establish the reliability of recommendations and to apply any resulting lessons.

Research and development

Regular monitoring of research and development expenditure is essential.

The plans will have established the purpose, phases, expenditure and timing of the programme, but they often turn out to have been optimistic and the results are much slower to emerge. The board must be aware of the position and its implications for the future of the business.

Manpower development

Nothing is more important to the progress of the business than the human resources at its command. For this reason, the assessment of performance, the development of manpower resources and management development plans are essentially the concern of the board.

The year-end hockey stick

This term has been applied to the pressure for year-end results. A pattern of fairly even trading during the first nine months of the year and then a surge of activity in the last quarter is quite common in businesses which stretch themselves to achieve goals. Efforts to maintain a smoother course often prove unsuccessful, and a great deal of planning and energy is devoted to achieving the target revenues at the end of the year. In most US corporations there is the same pressure to achieve quarterly results.

If a company is entering a period of intense activity in the closing three months of the year, there are certain things which need to be done:
- a careful analysis of order backlog which can be converted into billings before the year end
- a detailed review of prospects to determine which are probables for order

closure *and* conversion to billings before the year end
— thorough checks across the company to remove any obstacles to building and shipping the products up to the closing week of the year if prospects are converted to orders. This may involve establishing for this period a special 'operations room' following up daily on the prospects and order position, seeking opportunities for new sales activity, and keeping the factory closely informed as each situation develops.
— a weekly review of progress across the company by the managing director and a reprojection of quarterly results as the situation evolves.

The information can be presented in the following form:

	Forecast Q4 revenue	Backlog which can be billed in Q4	Orders required to book and bill in Q4	Original plan
Product A	450	250	200	500
B	500	300	200	700
C	300	150	150	200

One of the by-products is likely to be a reduced backlog going into Q1 of the new financial year. The plan, therefore, should be to aim consistently to raise the order level in order to satisfy the requirements of both current billings and the following year backlog.

Chapter 8

The Business is People

The skills involved in management are widely undervalued in the UK, and good management rarely receives the praise it deserves. Yet it surely cannot be denied that successful commercial management leads to growth, employment and investment, which is the aim of any industrial policy.

Is the ability to manage something some people are born with? To some extent, yes. Many people have natural qualities of leadership, drive and shrewdness which may be nurtured and developed in early life. But much of the practical skill of management, as of any profession, derives from training, education and hard work. That this fact is not widely recognised in the UK is one major reason why industry and commerce generally have done so little to attract educated talent, both graduate and postgraduate. The contrast with recruitment to the City, the Civil Service or the advertising world is considerable. In a number of other developed countries, management is certainly regarded more as a profession.

The best managers are those who have been able to cultivate their natural qualities of leadership and have worked hard to gain a thorough understanding of the principles of sound management.

Apart from understanding the interrelationship of skills needed in almost any business situation, the manager has to be able to work with people and through people. A single individual can have a dramatic effect on the fortunes of a business. A manager has to be able to recognise the special qualities of his subordinates and develop them, for a manager is only as good as his team.

The character of the company

The character of an organisation is determined by the board and personified in the chairman and the managing director.

The arguments for separating these two roles were put forward in Chapter 2. Many businesses need the 'thinker', concerned mainly with the development of strategy, and the 'achiever', who implements board policies and sees that things happen. This combination of personalities has proved successful many, many times. This does not, of course, imply keeping the chairman in an ivory tower. On the contrary, he must spend time in the operational areas if he is to be informed and effective. But he will express his wishes through his managing director.

The company character will, to some degree, also be influenced by and reflected by strong independent non-executive directors. They may well be particularly concerned with important customers at home and abroad and have external contacts of value to the company.

Organisation structure

The managing director achieves his objectives through an organisation structure. Too many layers of responsibility make the line of control too extenuated and the operational areas too remote for best results. Too few layers of responsibility mean that the managing director has too many managers reporting to him directly. The right structure is a matter of judgement depending on the particular business and the characteristics of the managers.

The general aim should be to decentralise into self-contained, self-accounting profit centres. There is evidence of best results being achieved if the operational unit is not in excess of 500/600 people. Such a unit is small enough for people to know each other but large enough to be self-managing while still able to obtain specialist help from the corporate centre or from external advisers. Many organisations go further on the road to decentralisation, either by complete management 'buy-outs' or by joint venture. The aim is to spread the profit responsibility and capital motivation. The big difficulty in large organisations — and particularly in nationalised industries or the Civil Service — is that there is no real risk of financial failure, and apparently no real recognition of 'bottom line' philosophy and responsibility.

To decentralise in this way does not mean to abandon control. The management skill lies in permitting maximum freedom to the operating units, while ensuring they are working to the policies and guidelines of the board. Regular monitoring of performance is, of course, necessary, but this is done using the same information as that produced by the unit for its own purposes. Not all managing directors find it easy to stand back in this way. The role is essentially different from managing a single unit. Take, for instance, the case of a group of restaurants or hotels. The manager of a single unit may be outstanding at his job, where he is in direct contact with the operational staff and the customers. Promotion to a co-ordinating role might not suit him at all. Many managers find this kind of transition difficult and may be wise never to attempt it. To work through other managers requires a totally different style and approach, for which training and preparation are necessary.

The judgement that a manager is not performing well is often a difficult one to make. It may be that his own manager has not performed as well as he should, and there is a risk the wrong man may be taking the rap. That is why performance should be measured as far as possible against agreed objectives. But of course personalities cannot be ignored — they are probably the single most important factor in a working environment. Many managers are unfortunately not able to deal frankly with their subordinates — they try to avoid performance discussions, preferring to let matters go by default rather than risk personal challenge. The appraisal system should be designed to encourage an open relationship.

Job titles

It is a fact that most individuals are concerned about status, and a title is an indication of status. It may seem easy to give someone a title as a form of appeasement and to avoid a confrontation. But there is usually a price to be paid, sooner or later. It is therefore necessary to think carefully about titles, paying attention to their implications across the company.

The following are a few examples of how job titles can be used. 'Associate Director' is a useful title for recognising near-board status; the holder will reasonably expect promotion to director in due course, so don't give this title unless that is the intention. 'Director of Sales' implies that the holder is not a full director of the company. It is different from 'Sales Director'. There is a similar difference between 'Assistant to the Sales Manager' and 'Assistant Sales Manager'.

Although it is an administrative and financial nuisance, it is sometimes worthwhile forming subsidiary companies so that the status of a number of personnel can be satisfactorily recognised.

Establishing a policy on titles is well worth a bit of board time.

Executive appointments

Because a business is its management, the appointment of key executives and their performance are of fundamental importance. The wrong senior appointment is very damaging both in money and time. Once a senior appointment is made, it may be up to three years before assessments show it to have been unsatisfactory and a new appointment can be made. Such a length of time can be critical to market positioning and commercial success. The morale of other employees is usually adversely affected, and when confidence is low very little constructive work can be expected. Once the decision is made to change, therefore, it must be executed rapidly but with understanding. A bad senior appointment normally reflects as much on the appointer as on the executive himself. The greatest care should be taken to avoid this kind of mistake, especially when bringing in someone from outside.

Most successful companies have based their success on a management team rather than on a number of individual talents. It is therefore very important when considering a new appointment to think of the working environment and the people already established there. The position to be held in the organisation by the new appointee must be carefully considered. To whom will he report? Who will be reporting to him? With whom will he be working closely as a member of the executive team? Organisations have their own style — their own chemistry. Judging how well a person will fit in with that style is as important as evaluating his technical or managerial competence.

The successful management team is well balanced, with individuals contributing complementary skills of a high standard.

If an outside agency for executive search is to be used, it must be allowed time to gain a good understanding of the organisation's structure, products, business plans and, most importantly, its management, its style and its chemistry. The appointment process involves:

— defining the job carefully and in detail
— preparing a profile of the candidate sought, defining essential requirements
— describing the career development which the successful candidate could anticipate
— making sure that at least two people and preferably more, are responsible for the recruitment. Mistakes are bound to occur occasionally but a disciplined approach and complete understanding of the task will keep these to a minimum. When in doubt, it is probably a good princple not to proceed: gut reactions are important and should not be ignored — they are often right. Some people have a real flair for choosing the right person and those who make good appointments always succeed in broadening their own career prospects.

Recruitment is critical to business performance, and senior management has to devote a good deal of time to deal with it. There is a widespread reluctance to give this aspect of business adequate attention.

Line and staff functions

It is necessary here to ask the difference between a 'line' job and a 'staff' job. A line manager carries direct responsibility for profit and achievement of business objectives. A staff manager essentially has the role of adviser to the line manager (although, of course, he almost always has his own subordinates for whom he carries direct responsibility). Thus, the sales manager and production manager have line jobs, whereas the financial and personnel functions are essentially staff.

The organisation must have a clearly understood network of responsibility from the board to the lowest operational level.

The line operational command goes direct from the principal executive manager to the work force, through subordinate managers.

The personnel function is perhaps the one which gives rise to most confusion, because it is dealing on a day-to-day basis with company employees in so many respects. This can give rise to the impression that the personnel manager is the boss of all the company personnel rather than just those in his own department.

The development of trade union organisations has complicated the picture. Many union members regard their trade union as their employer and respond more to its instructions than to those of the real employer. Employers themselves seem in some cases to have abrogated their responsibility of management. The best example of this is in the nationalised industries where consumers' interests are frequently trampled on. The result of operating as a monopoly without commercial pressure to perform effectively, and with powerful, closed-shop, tort-free trade unions, is that employees have lost sight of their only purpose for being there – to satisfy the customers.

Marketing is another area where lines of authority tend to get confused. Marketing and selling are not the same job, and any manager charged with looking after both is essentially performing two different roles. The marketing manager has to coordinate many other functions, and product managers get heavily involved in operational areas. Confusion can easily arise and should be avoided. The line organisation works best and carries the greatest respect if it is the only line of authority. This means making a conscious effort to support the line managers, and not to do things which weaken or destroy that authority.

One of the most common ways of destroying authority is to allow instructions to reach the shopfloor (or equivalent work area) through other channels. This is extremely damaging to good management. The foreman, traditionally one of the key members of a line management team, has had his authority eroded, with damaging consequences for the effectiveness of the work area: a strong shop stewards' organisation with, perhaps, different loyalties and objectives, has often played a part in this process.

The correct handling of communications is the key to the proper functioning of the organisation. It may be tempting for a managing director to use the staff newspaper to issue operational instructions. But it is quite essential that all members of line management know about it first, and are able to act with the necessary authority at the time. Staff bulletins or newspapers can perform a back-up role later.

Some organisations pay too little attention to dealing with employees and organising them correctly. It is perhaps the most important concern of the managing director, demanding a substantial part of his time. Many managers instead spend too much time on things which interest them more. No army commander would fall into that trap, because he knows what, in the final analysis, wins and loses battles.

An example of a simple organisation structure is shown in Figure 8.1. It is generally considered that four to six directly subordinate managers is a wide enough span of control, but circumstances can vary substantially.

Figure 8.1. *A simple organisation structure*

Another source of misunderstanding is the relationship of a staff function to its corresponding function at a subordinate level (eg finance and personnel in the diagram above). It is perfectly proper for a functional relationship to work on a 'dotted line basis', that is, without a line of command. The only real authority for a subordinate staff manager is his own line manager: but in practice it is necessary for one level to work closely with another on functional matters. Good communication and an understanding by all concerned of the principles involved are the keys to avoiding difficulties.

Nothing said here should preclude the right of a senior manager to talk to employees down the line. Indeed it is important for him to stamp his personality on the organisation in this way and not to rely on other managers or written 'blurbs'. He must visit the work area, see and be seen, and get a feel of the organisation. He must always, except in emergency, issue instructions through the proper line of authority. Although some of this may sound formal it is acceptable as long as the roles and principles are understood and accepted by the management team, and that those in authority have earned the respect of their subordinates — and vice versa.

Job descriptions

Any structure requires a proper understanding by each employee of his position in the team, to whom he is responsible and for what. Each job description needs to define carefully the general function, specific tasks, working relationships and limitations on authority.

Appendix 13 shows an example format for a job description. They should be kept fairly brief.

Performance appraisal

A system of performance objectives should be in operation throughout the organisation. This has five principal merits:

1. Board and managing director know how it is intended that the organisation shall fulfil its plans.
2. Those charged with responsibility for achieving objectives are involved in setting them; this ensures that the objectives are realistic and acceptable and that there is maximum commitment to achieving them.
3. The formulation of objectives forces the senior manager to think through how his own tasks are to be achieved and limits his ability to avoid responsibility if things begin to go wrong.
4. Objectives are a basis for measuring success or failure. In regular progress reviews, reasons for failure to reach objectives can be properly explored in face-to-face discussion.
5. Objectives make for better communication and direction throughout the organisation. In the process of setting them there is an upward flow of ideas, comments and proposals for improvement. If proposals are rejected reasons for doing so must be given, and ideas must never just get lost. It is important for people to feel that their opinions count.

Objectives should, wherever possible, be specific. For example: 'To achieve a ratio of net pre-tax profit to capital employed (as defined) of 33% by 31 December 19—.' Philosophical statements, or open-ended generalities, should be avoided: 'To improve the public image of the x activity' is, for instance, capable of many interpretations. The parties must agree the criteria by which satisfactory performance will be judged.

The essential elements in this form of appraisal are:

— the setting and agreement of key objectives
— agreeing the date by which each objective is to be achieved
— agreeing the criteria by which achievement will be assessed
— reviewing progress together regularly and periodically.

Other forms of appraisal are usually used in addition to this: some supplementary information may be needed from time to time. But the system of objectives and action plans should be operated throughout the organisation.

Such a system does not require a great deal of administration. The number of objectives for each individual should be quite small — only those judged to be very important to satisfactory performance of the job. From discussion of progress, it should emerge what actions the assessor might take to assist in the attainment of the objectives. The discussion is also likely to cover what needs to be done to improve performance or to assist in personal development.

If more formal annual assessments are required, they flow quite smoothly from the work already done during the course of the year. Such a formal review may be widened to include the next senior line manager and possibly the manager responsible for personnel.

It is often useful for the subordinate manager to propose his own objectives for discussion and to provide brief formal reports on progress against them. This kind of assessment is very positive and requires full involvement by both parties to what is, after all, a joint responsibility.

Career development

Performance reviews provide an opportunity to discuss a manager's career aspirations, possible ways of widening his experience or of extending his theoretical knowledge by attending courses, and so on.

The career development of his people is a key responsibility of any manager. There are many ways in which this can be done, but personal example and guidance in daily affairs figure high on the list. Courses may be of limited value, unless followed by an opportunity to use the newly gained knowledge in a practical situation. There is a danger too of a person returning from a course of training or development brimful of confidence and eager to put his new skills into practice and to be totally frustrated by his manager who has not had the same advantage or by an organisation which has no wish to adapt itself to new practices. Great care needs to be exercised, therefore, in the selection of the course to be attended, and the skills and experience of the trainer.

'Cross-posting' to give broader experience of different businesses is of great benefit but also difficult in practice. It is often easiest to arrange at general manager level. If it happens early in the career, there will be useful experience of other business activities and therefore wider general knowledge, but in a multi-product group it is difficult to appoint junior management into an actual operating situation; there is little value for the aspiring manager in just 'sitting by Nelly'.

There is growing alarm on the part of those concerned with business management about the absence of adequate training and development throughout UK industrial and commercial enterprises. The fact is that the UK does not put the effort or resources into commercial preparation that many of our principal competitors do — and the gap is not trifling but very significant. This is not essentially a government task, although the government does have a role to play. The responsibility lies squarely with the community at large — which seems economically illiterate — and of course with industry and commerce. In companies this requires in the first place an understanding at board level of the issues which confront them in this important challenge.

Some companies as a matter of policy rely on recruiting those perceived to have been trained by others, thus avoiding any direct responsibility in this respect. This may be a valid policy, but it is one which creates an imposition on others and means that the totality of effort is inadequate.

Perhaps even more worrying is the absence of sufficient in-depth educational competence in schools and in higher education. The number of graduates suitably educated for business and those with business degrees is quite inadequate to create a professional managerial structure able to compete on equal terms with international rivals. If this problem is not understood and soon resolved, any reversal in the UK's commercial and industrial decline over nearly a century is difficult to imagine. The best all-round training for a young manager is to be given control of some quite small operation which does not represent a big risk to the organisation if it does not work out well. Once a general management job has been held and performed successfully, it is much easier to develop a career pattern; and, if his present employer is not helpful in this, the manager is likely to find himself a more progressive environment in which to work. The manager who is motivated to do this is just the one not to lose!

With the aim of making the most of talent, some form of special advancement programme can be devised to ensure that outstanding people are offered the right challenges. The managing director of any sizeable organisation should aim to identify and develop good managers, and keep their progress under regular review.

Routine personnel reports

It is necessary to have records showing the structure of the staff by age categories, the retirement profile, the growth requirements, turnover of staff by function, and so on. Regularly collected data on these subjects are used to detect internal trends and for comparison with similar organisations. Jobs may well need to be graded, but care should be taken that the system remains flexible; the ability of the organisation to pay and the market situation, in particular, must be monitored and taken into account. Broad job comparability is not impossible, but it is very difficult to devise a scheme which can be applied across quite different operating acitvities. It is wise to have reports, once or twice a year, of total staff engagement costs. The direct costs are high: the hidden costs perhaps more so.

Employment contracts

Employment contracts are based on common law and modified by statute, particularly the Employment Protection (Consolidation) Act 1978.

In summary, the law requires that an employee who works for not less than 16 hours a week (or for the same employer for not less than five years and not less than eight hours a week) shall be given a written statement — which is not necessarily a contract — which must include as a minimum, the following:

- the identity of the parties
- the job title
- reference to any previous employment which will count as 'continuous'
- starting date of the employment
- terms, method and frequency of payment
- times and conditions of working hours
- holidays
- sickness
- pensions
- period of notice
- rates and regulations relating to the employment
- appeals machinery
- grievance procedure.

An employee is one who is employed as part of the business and his work is done as an integral part of it. This must be distinguished from a contract for service which, although done for the business, is not an integral part of it. The employee must, as a general rule, perform his tasks in the manner established by the employer.

Employers are required not to discriminate between employees, and must observe the Equal Pay Act 1970, the Sex Discrimination Act 1975 and the Race Relations Act 1976.

Under the Employment Protection Act, where an offence is committed by a company with the consent or connivance of, or neglect by, a director or senior officer, such person may be held personally liable as well as the company itself.

Some aspects of employment conditions are set out in Appendix 14.

The Truck Acts

Legislation in the nineteenth century known as the Truck Acts, the latest in 1896, was intended to protect manual workers and shop assistants from abuses in relation to deductions from wages, payments in kind and obligations to purchase goods from shops owned by employers.

In essence, the Truck Acts make illegal, null and void any payments of wages otherwise than in current coin of the realm. To the extent that variations are permitted under the acts, they must be in writing and also fair and reasonable.

Although on the statute book for nearly 100 years, there was an interesting recent case determined in favour of an employer who had made deductions from wages, in accordance with the contract of employment, in respect of till shortages on a garage forecourt. The court held that such deductions must be distinguished from a fine (which must be a sum certain), with the consequence that Section 1 of the 1896 Act was held not to be applicable, but that Section 2 dealing with compensation to the employer, was. But whereas Section 1 relates to shop assistants, Section 2 does not, and the employee was unsuccessful in his claim because no offence had in fact been committed under the legislation.

Employee involvement

In companies employing more than 250 people the Employment Act 1982 requires directors to state in their report to the shareholders the arrangements made to introduce, maintain or develop employee involvement, particularly in the following areas:

- providing employees systematically with information of concern to them
- consulting employees on a regular basis so that their views can be taken into account when making decisions likely to affect their interests.
- encouraging involvement in the company's performance
- achieving an awareness on the part of all employees of those financial and economic factors affecting the performance of the company.

These are wide-ranging issues about which companies need to develop policies and ensure that they are properly implemented.

In fact, directors of all companies, whatever their size, should realise that action along these general lines is nothing but good management. Not to do so is both shortsighted and against the interests of the company.

Employee benefits

Various benefits may be available to some or all employees, over and above the basic pay for the job, including:

- bonus payments and profit sharing
- commissions

— company cars
— medical insurance
— medical and dental facilities
— sick pay
— discounts on company products
— accommodation.

Pensions and share option schemes are, of course, also very important elements in remuneration packages. Personal taxation considerations affect nearly all employment benefits.

It is necessary to look at the total remuneration package before attempting comparisons or pricing a job.

Bonus payments and profit sharing

The essence of bonus payments should be to motivate and improve effectiveness. Bonuses that come with the rations — such as Christmas handouts — are given in the interests of general goodwill, but have very little effect on performance.

There are many ways in which bonus payments can be linked to greater efficiency, improved productivity or profits. In most cases a norm is agreed, and the bonus is applied to anything over the norm. This can be quite substantial, and there is no reason why up to 30 per cent or so of total basic remuneration cannot be in bonus form.

Examples of bonus arrangements include:

— bonus payable on company or departmental profits achieved in excess of budget requirement. The spread should favour management, because it is basically through management that improvements are brought about.
— bonus payments on improved labour productivity as evidenced by improved value added performance (see Chapter 7)
— bonus scheme related to earnings per share or profits per employee. The important thing is to make it relevant and identified with financial improvements, and accepted as credible by the employees.

For senior management a satisfactory bonus scheme can be built up from a number of factors, each of which is identified with the achievement of an agreed key objective. These may, for example, relate to orders, cash flow and profits (if these are the priority tasks) for each of which the bonus can be on a linear scale of 0 to 200 per cent with 100 per cent as target performance, as illustrated in Figure 8.2

		£ orders	£ bonus
Order intake	0%	75,000	0
	100%	100,000	2,500
	200%	125,000	5,000

Figure 8.2. Bonus scheme based on orders

In addition, there can be a discretionary element relating to important factors which may not be quantifiable, such as implementing a satisfactory computer system in a particular area by a certain date. The total bonus package could perhaps be composed as in Figure 8.3.

	% of total bonus
(a) achievements against financial objectives: such as order intake, sales, cash, rate of turn of operating assets	50/60
(b) if appropriate, an element in respect of the achievement of group profits, of which the particular company is a part	15/20
(c) success in achieving key objectives not measurable on a financial basis	25

Figure 8.3. *A total bonus package*

Commissions

The general principle of making commission payments to those primarily motivated by sales performance is well understood, but careful thought is needed to develop the most effective scheme.

Where the salesman is dependent on others to close business, group bonuses may be appropriate; in any case commission should essentially be related to 'on target' performance and above.

The support given to a salesman by his wife can be recognised by gifts for her (release the catalogue ahead of time) or subsidised holidays. Be careful to clear tax implications before the event.

The provision of cars

This is a widely provided benefit in the UK. It depends basically on business mileage being in excess of 2,500 per year. Tax assessments are based on scale benefits set out in the Finance Acts. The avoidance of capital costs by the employee is of substantial advantage. As part of a total remuneration package, it may be tax effective to provide a second car for certain senior staff, bearing in mind that the benefit will be taxed on the individual at 150 per cent of scale rate.

The provision of accommodation

In general, living accommodation provided because of employment is a taxable benefit based on the rental value (or rent paid if higher) of the property. There are some exceptions of a specialised nature. Homes costing over £75,000 also give rise to a tax benefit calculated on the notional interest on the excess cost.

Pensions

There is a wide variety of pension schemes arranged by employers over and above the state pension scheme. The benefits can vary significantly between one scheme and another: in some the employee makes a contribution, in others the contributions are paid wholly by the company. There is an Inland Revenue pension limit of two-thirds of final salary and minimum service of 10 years. Some schemes provide for a proportion of the employee's pension to be payable to the spouse; some provide an element of minimum annual increase after retirement.

Changes in pension arrangements are currently being considered by the government, including improved pension benefits for leavers and the availability of 'personal pensions'.

Employees may be able to improve their pension arrangements by making additional voluntary contributions.

In lieu of, or in addition to, the normal pension scheme it is possible to arrange pensions which benefit particular employees or categories of employees, including directors. For example, quite substantial lump sums can be set aside at say, the year end, and applied to the benefit of the target category, perhaps replacing bonuses or dividends. Such arrangements can be tax effective.

Pension benefits arising from such schemes are aggregated with other pension benefits and are therefore subject to the usual Inland Revenue limitations applied to approved pension schemes.

The introduction of any pension scheme should not be undertaken without proper professional advice.

Because the performance of pension schemes is important to employees and to the finances of the company, management of pension funds should be most carefully considered and, in general, the appointment of a professional investment manager is preferable to 'self-administration'. Either way, a professional monitoring service should be arranged so that the company and the trustees may know how the performance of their fund compares with that of other schemes and the causes of variation.

If a professional investment manager is to be appointed, as much care should be taken as with the engagement of any consultant or executive. Start with a careful selection of, say, three or four managers, based on performance over at least the previous five years – the more sophisticated advisers can readily provide this information. Then prepare a summary of the key facts relating to each applicant; compare their performance, particularly the number of times each has not been within the upper quartile of performers and the annual and cumulative rates of return achieved by the funds under their management. Then invite the applicants to submit a written proposal, including their specific recommendation for the company's actual portfolio (if it already exists). Finally, put together a panel of trustees and advisers and interview each applicant. It will be surprising if a very good investment manager does not emerge from this process.

Finally, sensible communication and consultation arrangements with employees is important. There is considerable ignorance at all levels about this complex but valuable benefit. Amongst other arrangements, there should be an employee consultative committee and pre-retirement counselling.

Share options

A share option grants a right to the holder to acquire shares in the company at a pre-agreed price. It may be an option against existing shareholders, but it is more likely to be against the company to be satisfied from unissued shares.

Option schemes have been widely recognised outside the UK as providing strong management motivation to create profitable companies. They offer the opportunity to create private wealth without the need for personal capital resources. The benefits accrue to the community, the company and the successful individual alike. Nevertheless, there has been considerable resistance in the UK to recognising these commercial virtues and, until recently, a hostile tax regime.

Until the Finance Act 1984 the tax implications of share options were strongly discouraging: personal taxation rates became payable on the 'gain' in value at the time the option was exercised. The gain was calculated by deducting from the market value (or negotiated market value) of the shares the price paid for the shares and, if applicable, the price paid for the option. This heavy taxation penalty considerably reduced the benefit and, therefore, the motivational value.

The Finance Act 1984 has changed all that. For Inland Revenue approved schemes, it is now possible to arrange share options so that taxation is on the basis of capital gains tax (not personal tax) and becomes payable only when shares issued against the option are realised. The key conditions for approval are:

- maximum value of option at time of issue is £100,000 or 4 × emoluments
- the option price at time of grant must approximate to the market value of the shares
- the option cannot be exercised earlier than three years or later than ten years after grant
- at the time of grant, the option holder must be a full-time employee (this includes directors)
- exercise of option can only take place once every three years
- option holders may not have a material interest (10 per cent) in the company
- options are non-transferable and must relate to fully paid ordinary shares.

All companies would be well advised to consider the benefits of introducing such a scheme, intended primarily for managers, executives and directors.

SAYE share option schemes

The Finance Act 1980 introduced the concept of encouraging wider share ownership by employees in their company through approved savings related option schemes. The financial conditions are:

- a maximum permitted monthly contribution
- the share price at which the option can be exercised may not be less than 90 per cent of market value when the option is granted
- a restriction against participation if the holder controls more than 25 per cent of the shares and it is a close company
- the money to purchase the shares must be saved through a special SAYE contract aimed to realise the required cost of the shares at its maturity
- earlier exercise of the option only under special circumstances (eg death, retirement, redundancy).

Schemes established in conformity with the legal requirements are tax-free. When the shares are sold capital gains tax will apply to the excess of any sale proceeds over the their investment cost.

Other schemes

From 1972 onwards it has been possible to provide share incentive schemes and since 1979, profit sharing schemes with varying taxation consequences.

Complicated taxation provisions apply to benefits arising, or deemed to arise, in the case of directors or higher paid employees, as a result of the acquisition of shares in a company by reason of employment.

Communications

A very real benefit flowing from the system of managing through objectives (as described above, p116) is the development of communications throughout an organisation. The absence of really effective communication is a shortcoming in many organisations. There should be a constant requirement and encouragement right from the top to the free flow of ideas both upwards and downwards. A senior director should be assigned special coordinating responsibility for all communications – internal and external. This may be the chairman and/or the managing director, but not necessarily so.

A properly considered communications plan developed by the board should include keeping all employees informed about the company and its progress. Communication with employees is an essential responsibility of all management and it certainly cannot be discharged by using a trade union structure as its mouthpiece.

There may be various communication channels used by employees, the principal one being through line management whose authority must be maintained. Other channels of communications include:

— staff newspapers (which must have quite clear purposes)
— pension scheme reports to members
— annual accounts report (probably specially written for employees)
— presentation and/or conferences (an opportunity for senior management to talk direct to employees)
— current trading information (visual display units can be used to disseminate important current information immediately).

External communications need just as much detailed thought, to present in the most favourable light the company philosophy, objectives and character. Advertising and PR plans clearly play an important role, but there are various supplementary means of reinforcement, for example:

— the annual report
— national and local press materials and, occasionally, presentations
— trade press communications
— design of street trading premises and displays
— for companies quoted, or preparing to be quoted, on the Stock Exchange or USM, a plan is needed to gain public and City understanding with a view to securing a fair share price and marketability.

Design

Closely related to communication is image. It is very desirable that there should be a strong design concept approved by the board which distinguishes the business from all others and leaves a clear message about the organisation. The director responsible for communication might very well also be in charge of design.

Work improvement performance

Work study – or time and motion study – is established practice in manufacturing activities. It is important to remember to keep the measurement methods up-to-date. Whenever changes are made in the factory or workshop, some adaptation is likely to be necessary. If this is not done, costing data and performance measurement become more and more remote from what is happening in practice. Put the item on the checklist for regular review – perhaps quarterly or half-yearly.

Much less well established is the application of the same principles to the office, particularly where there is a substantial clerical element. And yet it can be just as effective as in the plant. Here is an example of how it worked some years ago in a medium-sized firm which depended on a substantial clerical element.

After some debate and a good deal of preparation, the managing director was persuaded to invite consultants who specialised in this type of work to study the problem and submit a feasibility report. Before even looking at the job, the consultants said that they would be very surprised if a manpower reduction of at least 20 per cent could not be achieved, because they knew from experience that this was par for the course in any company. This claim met with scepticism, but in due course the consultants were appointed. They undertook the work only on the basis that the staff would be assured that there would be no redundancy; without this assurance it would not have been possible to obtain their co-operation. The managing director remained extremely doubtful but, to his credit, fully supported the work — another essential element in success.

Three years later the company had achieved its target of 20 per cent reduction in manpower, and the whole staff were working more effectively and with more purpose. Regular consultation between managers and supervisors took place to review actual performance against target; consequently there was far more communication about the work, and therefore about company performance, than had previously been the case. Within five years the company was operating with a staff some 60 per cent of the original level, with perhaps a slightly reduced business volume, at a cost of something like £15,000 in consultancy fees. At £5,000 per head employment cost this meant that basic running costs had been permanently reduced by about £500,000 per annum.

This experience shows how little credibility should be attached to the opinions of managers that economies cannot be effected without adverse consequences. Similarly, statements by local government officials, government departments or union leaders that cutting expenditure must result in reducing services are always very questionable. The results are likely to be best in large clerical operations, but the method can also succeed in smaller specialised departments.

Resistance from managers can be expected, partly because some think that if successful the results will reflect badly upon them. Such fears must be dispelled. If the work is not genuinely supported from the top of the organisation, the best results will invariably not be achieved. In the case referred to earlier, once it could be seen that the work was going ahead satisfactorily, and there was no revolution, the managing director become wholly convinced by the concept. The business subsequently went 'on line' with its computer systems, and the working methods naturally had to be reviewed and reassessed. This time there was no need for consultants.

Appraisal testing

Although not very widely practised, appraisal testing has a real part to play when considering whether the aptitude, personality and skills of an individual are likely to match those required in the job. It is an additional insurance against making mistakes when employing new people. But it can also be valuable in assessing employees' suitability for promotion or for training and development. The aim of appraisal testing is to avoid getting the square peg in the round hole. If a person's aptitude and temperament suit the job then that person will generally perform the work with enthusiasm. This means checking the person's all-round aptitude for the work and his temperamental ability to work with the existing senior staff. It is possible that more problems are caused by mismatching personalities than by lack of ability.

Appraisal testing can be used in assessing natural aptitudes for technical work such as word processing or computer operations or for the wider purpose of measuring supervisory or managerial aptitudes.

Appraisal testing is carried out by skilled practitioners who are able to measure individual characteristics against established norms built up from a wide range of tests in relation to several discrete criteria. The cost of the service is not particularly high and can be regarded as a reasonable price to pay if it assists in making the best use of a valuable resource — people. An example of the type of report which can be expected is given in Appendix 15.

Key man insurance

If a company's success is likely to be seriously affected by the loss or disablement of certain senior executives, or is very dependent upon, say, a technical manager who is responsible for an important research task, consideration should be given to protecting the company by taking out insurance cover. It is not expensive — particularly for death only — and will provide some compensation while the company makes replacement arrangements, especially important in smaller companies.

Standards of excellence

If you don't aim for excellence, it is very unlikely that your subordinates will. And if we don't learn to be professional about our business, how shall we compete with others who are?

Achieving excellence is very difficult. It can only be done by practical example and a determination to succeed, day after day after day. It is hard work, and requires constant attention to detail. Setting and insisting on such standards may not lead to great popularity, but it probably will earn respect. The truth is that people do like to work for successful organisations and for managers who know where they are going and how they intend getting there. They do not need to *like* their managers. Many managers find it difficult to take the tough decisions and the unpopularity which may, in the short term, go with them. But employees usually recognise and accept very well the necessity to make such decisions, provided proper explanation is given and implementation is seen to be fair. Most of us look for leadership and are proud to belong to a successful outfit.

In mergers between companies different philosophies and standards become very apparent. And they are deep-rooted and take a long time and a great deal of effort to change. This is one reason why senior management changes may have to be made, and why senior managers prefer to have their own trusted team around them when they move into a different environment.

Chapter 9

Systems and Computers

The choices offered to the business manager by the rapidly changing computer technology are bewildering. In one decade, we have gone from mainframes, to minis and then to micros. Office automation bringing transaction processing and communications together in a single system is now available. Networking within the office and with the world outside is developing rapidly. The penetration of office procedures by increasingly sophisticated technology is bound to bring great changes in many routine business functions and in the work of managers themselves.

The availability of this technology and, particularly, the ease with which the micro can now be harnessed, has led to a solutions-oriented approach which is diverting attention from the development of effective systems strategies.

So what should be done?

Systems strategies

There are two key requirements which need to be taken account of in developing a systems strategy:

- the need for, and meaning of, timely, accurate and clear information relating to key activities
- the forward-looking role of management accounting.

The systems strategy must be designed to satisfy these requirements and it may or may not be computer based.

A systems strategy must be based on the basic business framework:

- the three- or five-year business plan
- the factors crucial to success in that plan
- the performance measures to be used to monitor progress.

Its focal point is not then economic return: that is, it does not have as its priority the need to justify itself in a cost effective sense (although this is important); instead it has a more imaginative business aim such as revenue enhancement (for example, measuring return on capital by product), competitive advantage or opportunity assessment.

Automation

Most businesses today use their computers for the narrow function of transaction processing, often in a somewhat ad hoc way, rather than in the context of an overall computer concept for the business. Automation of the information systems which measure the performance of the business in its key areas and provide the essence of control should underlie the determination of systems strategies.

The principal benefits flowing from automation of information include:

— accuracy
— speed of delivery
— comprehensiveness
— multi-transaction (eg, from cash till to stock records and sales analysis through a single system)
— real time
— rapid evaluation of options.

Analysis of management accounts will indicate the priorities for systems development.

Management control

Effective and properly planned systems development is increasingly important in terms of both cost effectiveness and opportunity enhancement. It is a key management task, and a director should be charged with the responsibility for development of policy and its successful implementation. The manager responsible for implementation may or may not be the chief financial manager: there are good arguments for appointing a manager for information systems, a much broader role than that attaching to the finance function, reporting directly to the managing director.

Information systems will have a central role in future business organisation. It is therefore an important policy area for the board to consider. The systems strategy could include the following elements:

— management information systems and management accounts
— decision support systems
— transaction processing systems
— payment systems
— accounting systems and financial accounts.

Bearing in mind the broad aims of a system, we now look in more detail at computer applications.

Management responsibility for computers

It is not necessary for managers to understand the intricacies of computers or how they work, any more than it is necessary for them to know how to keep a set of accounts. But just as they do have to understand the results of accountancy, and what the figures mean, they do have to understand what computers do and cannot do; they must recognise the vital part the computer has to play in developing appropriate systems. 'Leaving it to the computer man' is very risky.

It is essential that the manager as user is wholly involved in the project. Above all, he must be absolutely clear what he wants the system to do for him, and to be satisfied that, when authority is given to proceed, the results will meet his specification at an agreed time and cost. As in architecture, if the client starts to amend the specification along the road the results will almost certainly be less satisfactory and more costly.

To assess and limit the risks, disciplined procedures must be followed. Firstly, the manager must be quite clear what outputs he wants from the system in due course; they must be explained in the brief from which the computer experts will work out their solutions. Secondly, it is dangerous to look for a computer solution if a manual system has not already been developed. Many managers do not realise this problem.

Guidelines for computer projects

Because moving to computers has been, and is, a source of considerable difficulty, Appendix 16 sets out the step-by-step approach which was developed in the Hill Samuel merchant bank, for both new systems and operating systems. Sophisticated applications were being developed in banking, investment management and foreign exchange. Package solutions were not appropriate: this meant building a professional team to develop suitable programmes across a wide range of financial services. It is hoped that managers who are experiencing difficulties or approaching the problem for the first time will find the guidelines in Appendix 16 helpful.

The availability of off-the-shelf programs for minis and micros is substantially reducing both the risk and the time involved in installing computer systems, and it is these that most small businesses first encounter. Whatever computer is being considered, there are two fundamental principles:

- involvement and commitment by management as user
- professional project management by the technicians.

The cost-effectiveness of computers has been increasing for many years: the real costs have reduced every year. A marked trend towards distributed processing — the location of terminals or mini-computers in working areas — has taken place in the last decade. This is now being supplemented by the micro, and by the development of network capability to link micros together. And with these trends has come the availability of packaged programs so that applications are becoming much less risky. Even quite small businesses can now justify the purchase or leasing of a computer which will perform several accounting functions, offer word processing and listing capabilities.

The two wares

Computer systems comprise two basic ingredients. 'Hardware' is the term applied to the computer equipment itself. 'Software' is the term applied to the programming instructions to make the hardware perform. Because the computer cannot think, it will work only to its instructions, however stupid those may be. 'Garbage in, garbage out', as they say. The trend over the years has been for an increasing proportion of total cost to apply to the software. Remember also that there is a substantial annual maintenance cost for keeping the system up to date and developing new applications. An assessment of costs, therefore, should cover a period of years and encompass hardware, software, staff training, parallel running and maintenance. If it is assumed there will be staff substitution, be cautious and in any case do not overlook the costs of termination.

Security

The integration of computers into the business infrastructure brings with it new problems of security — for the equipment itself, for authority to enter the system, for the risks of fraud, for the consequences of computer failure, fire hazards and not least, failure of electricity supply. Each of these risks must be assessed and protective action considered. The purchase of a small generator may well prove to be a sound investment to ensure electricity supply. And standby facilities should be carefully considered, not necessarily in-house.

Financial modelling

Because of its ability to perform calculations very rapidly, the computer can, when properly programmed, be of great assistance to management in providing answers to questions which could otherwise not have been answered at all, or only at inordinate expense.

As a planning tool, therefore, the computer can be a considerable aid. Once the model of the business (or function) has been set up in mathematical terms, alternative scenarios can be considered by seeking solutions to the 'what if' questions. Thus, rather than formulating just one hypothesis, several different possibilities can be considered by management before taking final decisions on sensitive aspects of the business which can be very important to ultimate financial results.

Data Protection Act

The Data Protection Act became law in 1984. It has wide application and will affect many companies, which must have registered with the Data Protection Registrar within six months of 11 November 1985.

The essence of the legislation is that organisations which use data processing equipment to process information about 'data subjects' (individuals who can be identified from information recorded in a form which can be processed by equipment operating automatically in response to instructions given for that purpose) are required to register either as a data user (if the data processed are for their own use), or as a computer bureau (if the processing is for some other party). There are some exceptions, mainly in the public sector. The principal exceptions affecting the private sector are concerned with payroll or accounting purposes. But note, for example, that a debtors' ledger maintained on computer is caught by the Act.

The principles applicable to data records are:

— information shall be obtained fairly and lawfully
— personal data shall be held only for specified and lawful purposes
— personal data shall not be used or disclosed in any manner incompatible with the purposes specified.
— personal data shall be adequate, relevant and not excessive
— personal data shall be accurate and kept up to date
— personal data shall not be kept longer than necessary
— an individual shall be entitled to be informed whether any personal data are held; to have access to them; and, where appropriate, to have such data corrected or erased
— apppropriate security measures shall be taken against unauthorised access to, or alteration, disclosure or destruction of, personal data; and against accidental loss or destruction of personal data.

The act makes available compensation for damage and distress due to loss or unauthorised disclosure of data, or to inaccurate data.

The above principles are expected to become enforceable in November 1987. Responsibility for compliance with the act rests with the board. This they should discharge by appointing an officer responsible for the co-ordination of data protection, ensuring that the necessary steps are taken to conform with the requirements of the act.

Chapter 10

The Law and Business

Managers must have some understanding of the legal implications of business transactions, for it is not possible to conduct any business without creating contractual rights and obligations.

In the vast majority of cases, whether or not the legal aspects of a transaction have been properly understood is of little practical consequence. However, events never go smoothly all the time; there are bound to be misunderstandings, shortcomings, cases of bad faith. And on these occasions everyone looks to the law for help. If basic procedures have had insufficient regard for legal implications, then there is trouble. Difficulties frequently arise when discussions have taken place, but are not recorded either on internal files or in confirmatory documentation.

Contract

Every transaction implies a contract.

Contract law is based upon cases decided in court over hundreds of years. This 'common law' has been changed and supplemented by numerous acts of Parliament and statutory instruments.

A contract is an agreement enforceable by the law, between two or more persons, their intention being to create legal relations between them. The essence of such a contract is an offer; and an unconditional acceptance of that offer. An offer to negotiate is not an offer in the sense indicated, but an 'invitation to treat'. It may be noted that a contract is valid, whether in writing or not, although misunderstandings are much more likely in verbal contracts and proof in court is very difficult. Nevertheless, many commercial transactions, particularly in financial areas, do proceed on the basis of oral agreements, some of them very substantial.

Whether in writing (except under seal) or oral, the essence of a contract is the existence of consideration. Whilst this is usually a sum of money, it need not necessarily be so: 'An act of forbearance of one party or the promise thereof is the price for which the promise of the other is bought and the promise thus given for value is enforceable.' This definition of consideration was adopted in 1915 by the House of Lords in Dunlop v Selfridge.

Apart from those contracts which must be by deed, Parliament has enacted that certain other contracts must be in writing or evidenced in writing.

A company which is incorporated becomes a legal entity, quite separate and distinct from its members. It therefore carries on its activities through agents. Such a company need not contract under seal except when an ordinary person has to do so.

Because the company is brought into being through incorporation under the Companies Act, its powers are circumscribed under the Act itself and by the memorandum of association. Any act in excess of those powers is ultra vires and will be void. Hence great care is required in drafting the memorandum, and particularly the 'objects' clause within it. It may also be noted that the European Communities Act of 1972 is relevant to the ultra vires rule: its intention is to protect parties dealing in good faith with a company by deeming that transactions decided on by its directors are within the legal capacity of the company. It will be evident, however, that the effect may in fact be limited because of the words 'decided on by the directors'.

The law of contract is complicated, and beyond the purpose and scope of this book. However, it is appropriate to mention the question of misrepresentation, which can and frequently does arise. In effect, it means that one of the parties has entered into a contract on a false understanding, and that there has not therefore been genuineness of consent.

Misrepresentation can be broadly classified into three types: innocent, negligent and fraudulent.

The legal consequences and remedies differ in each case, but turn on rescission of the contract, or damages. If one of the parties has entered into a further contract with a third party before rescission takes place, that third party may also be affected. In such circumstances, the remedy will lie in damages.

Rescission involves putting the parties back into the position they were before the contract was made, as far as possible. Restitution, therefore, must also be made by the return of any benefits received under the contract by either party.

In commercial matters, it is frequently the case that, before contract, a process of exchange of information, enquiry, discussion, explanation and presentation by the seller takes place over a period of weeks or even months. Eventually, the sale is effected. If, in due course, difficulties arise because of a claim by one party or the other that the situation is not what had been expected or understood, it is not a simple matter to disentangle the true course of events and the statements which have been made in the exchanges leading to the transaction.

The remainder of this chapter attempts briefly to cover those aspects of commercial law which have been enacted by Parliament and are likely to have relevance in the normal conduct of almost any business.

Management needs to be aware of their existence if only for the purpose of knowing when it is wise to seek advice from the company lawyer. This is best done before accidents, not after, so that basic documentation and agreements are well drafted and understood as a matter of good commercial practice.

This will apply particularly when setting up a new business or when entering into new trades or types of transaction. A frequent cause of difficulty arises where transactions are being entered into which have the consequence of varying the basic agreements: there should be a firm procedure for written (or telexed) confirmation, and for the making of brief and dated file notes of what has been understood. These comments have special application when starting to trade in foreign countries where laws and practices as well as language are inevitably different from the UK.

Statute law, modifying or limiting the common law, particularly concerning consumer protection, has proliferated since the 1960s. A company's incorporation does not in any way reduce its responsibilities under this legislation. Moreover, directors may be individually liable to third parties for breach of contract or in tort, and also jointly and severally with the company for offences committed under particular statutes.

The personal exposure of a director to such a liability can arise from three basic causes:

- consent (ie he agrees to a course of action)
- connivance (ie knowing of a course of action, does nothing to prevent it)
- neglect (ie failing to take preventative steps).

The law extends this philosophy to 'any director, manager, secretary or other similar officer of a body corporate'. It is clearly impracticable for a director to be held personally liable in all circumstances. It is therefore important for the board to establish the necessary internal policies and procedures, so that it can be seen to be acting with proper regard to its responsibilities. Such responsibilities might well be discharged if the company has established:

- relevant policies
- internal procedures to give effect to policies
- training of employees in a proper understanding of the company requirements
- ensuring satisfactory internal reporting.

Although this may seem to be a further burden on the directors it can be looked at positively as the detailed attention which should be given by any responsible board to the complete satisfaction of its customers.

Sale of goods

The law relating to the sale of goods is to be found in the Sale of Goods Act 1979 which, of course, must be interpreted in the light of the common law.

A contract for sale of goods is a contract whereby the seller transfers, or agrees to transfer, to the buyer the property in goods in exchange for a money consideration.

The following are not within the scope of this act:

- a contract which does not pass ownership to the buyer (because property in goods implies ownership)
- money instruments and securities
- barter (because the consideration is not money)
- services
- an interest in land
- contracts for work and materials
- hire purchase (except when the hirer exercises his option to purchase at the end of the hiring period).

Some of these exclusions are specifically covered by the legislation.

The contract
The essential features of the contract are:

- The contracting parties must be of full capacity.
- There must be consideration. This usually means payment of money expressed

as a price (which however can be determined in a manner defined in the contract).

If a part payment is made at the time of entering into the contract, it is important to establish in the contract whether this is intended as a deposit or part payment, because ability to recover in the event of failure of the contract is different.

— If there is no agreement as to price, there is a presumption that a reasonable price shall be paid.
— The seller must deliver (ie voluntarily pass possession of) the goods. In the absence of agreement to the contrary the place of delivery is where the seller does his business or, in the case of specific goods (ie goods identified and agreed upon), where they are located if the buyer knew that fact when the contract was made. It is thus the buyer's responsibility to collect.
— The buyer is under obligation to pay when the seller delivers, in the absence of agreement to the contrary, provided that the delivery is strictly in accordance with the contract.
— Unless expressly stated that the exact time of delivery is the essence of the contract, the buyer cannot insist upon an exact time.

Conditions of the contract

Statements made in the course of negotiating a contract amount to representation. Reference has already been made to some of the consequences flowing from misrepresentations.

The terms of the contract may be either 'conditions' or 'warranties'.

A 'condition' is an important term of the contract. Breach of a condition allows the injured party to bring the contract to an end, and to sue for damages. A 'warranty', however, does not go to the root of the contract. It is less fundamental to the contract than a condition. The remedy for breach of warranty lies in damages only, but not in the rescission of the contract.

Implied terms of the contract

The Sale of Goods Act establishes that certain terms are implied in all contracts for the sale of goods, even if they are not specifically referred to:

— *Title*. The seller has a right to sell the goods, ie he either owns them or in the case of an agreement to sell, he will own them at the time the property is to pass. This is a 'condition'.

    The contract also implies that the buyer should hold the goods free of any third party charge and have quiet possession of them. These implied terms are deemed to be warranties, not conditions.
— *Description*. The goods must comply with the description given to them by the seller, who must describe them accurately. This is a condition.
— *Merchantable quality*. The essence of this implied condition is that goods sold in the course of business shall correspond with the quality and condition commonly expected of them (having regard to description, price and any other relevant circumstances). However, there may not be a breach of condition if defects are specifically drawn to the buyer's attention before contract or the buyer carried out an examination which should have revealed any defect.
— *Fitness for purpose*. Where the seller sells goods in the course of business and

the buyer (expressly or by implication) makes known to the seller (or to the dealer in a credit sale) the particular purpose for which goods are purchased, there is an implied condition that they are fit for that purpose. However, this may not apply if the purchaser did not in fact rely upon the skill and judgement of the seller, although reliance on the seller's skill and judgement will be readily implied in the case of sales to the general public as consumers. 'Usage of the trade' may also be relevant when interpreting intention of the parties.

— *Sale by sample.* The implied condition is that the bulk shall correspond with sample, that defects do not exist which would not be apparent from sample and that there shall be reasonable opportunity to examine bulk before delivery. If the sale is both by way of sample and description, both criteria must be satisified. The mere provision of a sample is insufficient: it must be shown that the parties intended the sale to be by sample.

By reason of the Unfair Contract Terms Act 1977 it is not possible for the seller to exclude any of the implied terms where the transaction is a 'consumer sale'. In other cases, some of the implied terms may be excluded in the sale contract, provided such exclusions are 'reasonable' (as defined by the act).

Two other points should be made. There is a duty on the seller supplying dangerous goods to warn the buyer of that danger. In addition, the Health and Safety at Work Act 1974 imposes a criminal liability on manufacturers who fail to give adequate information to enable their products to be used properly and with safety.

Other aspects of the Sale of Goods Act 1979

The act also deals with the consequences of breach of contract; the computation of damages to the injured party; the determination of exactly when property and risk pass from seller to buyer (affecting particularly insolvency and insurance); and the rights of a third party who purchases goods from a person who had no title to sell them.

It may be noted that where goods are purchased from a retailer, no action can be brought under the Sale of Goods Act by the purchaser against the manufacturer (since there is no contract between them). There may, however, be other remedies.

Title reservation by the seller

There is a growing trend by sellers to 'reserve title' to goods sold until paid for in full, thus attempting to retain some protection against the consequences of insolvency. Contracts should be carefully examined for such a clause. It is primarily aimed at securing precedence over creditors (particularly banks) rather than against the purchasing company. However, it is also usual for such clauses to specify identification of either the goods or the proceeds of sale and this imposes obligations on the purchaser in the conduct of his business to preserve that identification. This obviously presents practical diffuclties especially where goods purchased are changed in form through a manufacturing process. A well drafted reservation clause will impose 'risk' on the purchaser as from the time of delivery. The law is complex and not wholly clear on these issues.

It is worth noting that under the 1979 act a title reservation will not hold good against a third party buying in good faith and for value and without knowledge of the reservation.

Supply of goods and services

The Supply of Goods and Services Act became effective in 1982. It aims to give the same protection to the purchaser for the supply of goods in those cases which, whilst analogous to contracts of sale, were not in fact caught by the Sale of Goods Act.

Part I of the act concerns contracts for work and materials, exchange and barter, and hire. Maintenance and installation contracts are examples.

Hiring contracts are likely to fall into the following broad classifications:

— office equipment
— building and construction equipment
— goods hired by consumers
— motor vehicles.

Conditions broadly similar to those in the Sale of Goods Act are implied into such contracts and cannot be subverted by the supplier.

Part II of the act applies to a contract under which a person agrees to carry out a service, be it professional or otherwise. The act does not apply to contracts of service. Contracts for the supply of services in the course of business carry the following implied terms:

— The supplier must carry out the service with reasonable care and skill (ie with the care and skill of a reasonably competent member of the trade or profession).
— If a time for the service has not been fixed, the supplier must carry it out within a reasonable time. This is a matter of fact. In commercial contracts, time is of the essence unless otherwise determined in the contract, there is a waiver, or it is established by the course of dealings between the parties.
— If consideration for the service is not fixed by the contract, the beneficiary of the service must pay a reasonable price. This again is a matter of fact.

If some of these implied terms are excluded, the protective provisions in the Unfair Contracts Terms Act 1977 will come into effect, in particular liability for negligence and breach of contract.

Fair trading

The Office of Fair Trading, established under the auspices of the Director General of Fair Trading, has a wide ranging role designed in essence to protect consumers against trading practices which are considered unfair. Apart from its responsibility to consider company mergers involving assets of £30m or more (or creating a market share of at least 25 per cent) and to make recommendations to the Department of Trade and Industry with regard to monopolies and mergers, the Office of Fair Trading is concerned with a general raft of legislation aimed at trade practices which restrict, distort or prevent competition in the UK:

— The Fair Trading Act 1973

    — The Restrictive Trade Practices Act 1976
    — The Competition Act 1980.

There are many other statutes applying to particular products or classes of product which are relevant to businesses in those areas.

Trading is also affected by EEC legislation. The Treaty of Rome 1973, particularly Articles 85 and 86 affecting restrictive trade practices, is concerned with the distortion of competition and the abuse of a monopolistic position within the EEC. Breach of the treaty under these articles renders an affected agreement void. Enforcement lies with the Director General for Competition in the European Commission.

The Fair Trading Act 1973

Reference has already been made to the power given to the Office of Fair Trading in relation to mergers and monopolies. The 1973 act applies more generally to consumer protection against unfair trading practices. Here the Office of Fair Trading works with Trading Standards Consumer Protection departments and advice agencies; it provides information concerning consumer rights; where appropriate, it has power to seek assurances as to compliance with the law.

The Fair Trading Act empowers the Office of Fair Trading to negotiate codes of practice with trade associations. Many such codes have been agreed, but it must be recognised that they are voluntary. As they cannot be enforced by law, the power is significantly limited since those most likely to perpetrate offensive practices are least likely to have regard to the codes.

Restrictive Trade Practices Act 1976

The effect of this act is to require registration with the Director General of Fair Trading of collective agreements between two or more parties which are intended to fix prices and/or to regulate supplies of goods or services. The consequence of registration is to render the contract void and unenforceable unless the parties can prove to the Restrictive Trade Practices Court that the agreement satisfies one of the eight statutory conditions and is therefore deemed not to be against the public interest.

The practical consequence of this legislation is that many restrictive agreements, when threatened, are voluntarily terminated.

It may be noted that, to avoid evasion of the Restrictive Trade Practices Act, agreements to exchange information in relation to prices and/or the supply of goods are also liable to registration, with the same consequences.

The Resale Prices Act 1976

This act prohibits agreements intended by suppliers to impose minimum resale prices on purchasers, and makes it unlawful for a supplier to withhold supplies from a purchaser who refuses to adhere to the seller's restrictive price conditions. There is an exception in the case of goods sold as 'loss leaders'.

Such agreements are presumed void unless the supplier can prove that the restriction is in the public interest.

The Competition Act 1980

The principal thrust of this Act is to subject a company (or the group of which it is a member) which is neither a statutory monopoly nor within the scope of the Restrictive Trade Practices Act 1976 as being party to a collective agreement, to investigation by the Director General of Fair Trading. A company with a turnover of less than £5m is exempt unless it has a share of not less than 25 per cent in the relevant market.

Enquiries, if initiated, follow a two-stage process:

— by the Director General to determine whether the company is engaged in an anti-competitive practice and, if so, whether there should be a reference to the Monopolies Commission.
— by the Commission to confirm such a determination and, if so, whether the offence operates against the public interest.

As a result, the company can be directed to discontinue or amend the offending practice, or to give undertakings to this effect.

A person is deemed to engage in an anti-competitive practice, if, in the course of business, he pursues a course of conduct which, of itself or when taken together with conduct pursued by associated persons, has or is intended to have or is likely to have the effect of restricting, distorting or preventing competition in connection with the production, supply or acquisition of goods or services in the UK.

This Act is essentially concerned with effect, not intent.

Consumer protection

There are several pieces of legislation which deal with consumer protection; the following have particular relevance.

The Consumer Protection Act 1961

This act empowers the Trade and Industry Secretary to issue regulations specifying standards to which affected goods must conform if they are to be lawfully sold in the UK. Some 20 regulations have been so issued. A non-conforming sale is a criminal offence.

A person who seeks to exclude the enforcement of the regulations or to limit his liability through exclusion clauses in a contract will not be successful.

There are exceptions to the scope of the act, particularly where goods are not sold in the course of business, and in the case of exports.

The Consumer Safety Act 1978

This act operates in a similar manner to the Consumer Protection Act. It deals with goods which are the subject of government regulations prescribing standards to which they must conform if they are to be lawfully sold.

The Unsolicited Goods and Services Act 1971

The common law requirement that a contract cannot arise without an offer and acceptance (which cannot be implied by silence) is strengthened by the provisions of this act. It deals principally with the following:

— sending unsolicited goods
— demands or threats regarding payment for such goods
— entries in directories, unless previously authorised in writing

— sending unsolicited books, magazines or leaflets which describe human sexual techniques.

Consumer credit

The Consumer Credit Act 1974 replaces previous legislation dealing with money-lenders, pawnbrokers and hire purchase traders. This act is now fully in force, and is intended to regulate credit so that the law does not favour any one form of credit supply rather than another.

Borrowings may take the form of:

— restricted use agreements, where the borrowing may be applied to a specified purpose.
— unrestricted use agreements, where the borrowing may be applied to any purpose.

The Consumer Credit Act 1974 applies where:

— total credit does not exceed £15,000 and
— the hirer is not a corporation.

This is known as a regulated agreement. In all other cases the common law applies.

There are exceptions to the act, particularly transactions relating to land mortgages, export credits, building societies and loans carrying an interest rate of 13 per cent or less (or 1 per cent above the clearing bank base rate if higher).

In order to carry on a business offering financial arrangements within the scope of the act, a licence must be obtained from the Office of Fair Trading, which maintains a public register. To trade without a licence is a criminal offence.

Hire purchase

A hire purchase agreement allows the hirer possession of the goods and the right to use them in consideration for the payment of rental (usually by instalments) with an option to the hirer to acquire the goods for a nominal consideration at the end of the hiring period.

It is often the case in hire purchase that there is a connected lending agreement. This arises when a credit supplier (eg source of finance) advances money by way of loan to a purchaser to enable him to buy goods from a supplier. This is a connected lending agreement but the supplier and debtor have no direct contractual relationship. A direct loan from a finance house is not a connected lending agreement.

The agreement between finance house and supplier is essentially that of buyer and seller, although the retailer may also in some respects be an agent for the finance house.

It can be the case that the supplier is required to give a guarantee to the finance house; for self-protection, the supplier will then require the debtor to obtain a guarantor of his debt to the supplier. The act makes specific provisions in connection with the rights and obligations of guarantors.

There is a statutory cooling-off period, of not less than seven days, during which the debtor is entitled to rescind the agreement.

Finance leases

Sometimes known as equipment leases, these are distinguished from hire purchase agreements in that there is no option to purchase and goods must be returned to the hirer at termination. Such agreements to hire goods usually extend to the whole of their useful lives.

Short-term hirings of equipment, sometimes known as operating leases are clearly of a different nature.

Equipment leases are frequently used for the supply of vehicles, office machinery and computers.

Supply of Goods (Implied Terms) Act 1973

Both hire purchase and finance lease agreements are normally very comprehensive and detailed. This act deals with matters not expressly referred to in the agreements.

In the case of consumer transactions, the rights given by the implied terms cannot be excluded or restricted. In the case of business transactions, an exclusion clause will hold good provided it is reasonable.

Taxation

In hire purchase or conditional sale transactions, the hirer can claim the benefit of capital allowances as if the goods had been purchased, in respect of the capital element of the contract. In a credit agreement, however, taxation relief is available to the purchaser only at the time each instalment is paid.

Finance leases are different. In this case the finance house is the owner of the equipment and therefore is entitled to claim the benefit of capital allowances. However, it is frequently the case that some of that benefit will be reflected in the terms of payment under the lease. Such benefit will, of course, be of decreasing value following the changes to capital allowances in the Finance Act 1984.

Trade descriptions

The Trade Descriptions Acts 1968 and 1972 apply to statements, whether oral or written, made in the course of trade, relating to goods, services and certain pricing practices. It is an offence for anyone, in the course of business, to apply a false trade description of a material nature to any goods, or to supply or offer to supply any goods to which a materially false trade description is applied.

A trade description is briefly defined as any statement relating to goods concerning quantity, size or gauge; method of manufacture, production or processing; composition of product material; fitness for purpose or performance characteristics; other physical characteristics; claims concerning independent testing or seals of approval; place or date of manufacture, production or processing; the name of the manufacturer or producer and any claimed history of previous use.

The application of the act to pricing practices should be noted; in particular, false indications that a price is equal to or less than a recommended price or equal to or less than the seller's previous price. Unless specifically refuted by a contrary statement there is a presumption that in the case of price reductions, goods have been on offer at the higher price for a continuous period of not less than 28 days within the previous six months.

In 1972 the act was extended to imported goods: goods carrying or purporting to carry a UK name or mark must carry a statement as to their country of origin in a conspicuous place.

Intellectual property

The term intellectual property relates principally to:

– patents	Handled by registered patent agents. There are also trade
– trade marks	mark agents.
– registered designs	
– copyright	Normally handled by solicitors.

The rights arising from each of these properties are capable of transmission and of being exercised against third parties.

Except in the case of copyright the relevant legislation provides for a statutory register – under the auspices of the Department of Trade and Industry. Although the rights attaching to these intangible assets may be of considerable value, they will often not be identified in a company balance sheet.

Patents

The grant of a patent gives the right to the owner for a period of 20 years to prevent others exploiting the invention on which the patent is based, the consideration for which involves its public disclosure and definition. A patent cannot be granted in respect of computer programs and know-how. The characteristics of patents are:

– There must be an invention
– It must be something new, ie which has not been disclosed before
– The invention must be ingenious.

A patent cannot be granted if the patent application is not filed until after the invention has been made public or if, for example, a new product has already been offered for sale.

The priority date is the date on which the first application to protect the invention was filed with the Patent Office. It may be up to four and a half years before a definitive patent is issued, although the Patent Office will publish the application within 18 months of priority date.

A grant will not be made or will be invalid if there is an earlier disclosure of a similar invention, known as 'prior art'.

The patent protection applies only in the UK unless steps are taken to apply for protection in other countries. Provided such applications are filed within a year of the priority date, their protection will be retrospective to that date. In Europe it is possible to obtain patents in up to 10 European countries by applying through the European Patent Office. The search for wide international protection is expensive. It involves initial registration fees and annual renewal fees if the patent is to remain valid. Various commercial aspects of patenting need to be considered:

– Because of their potential importance to a business, the control of all patent processes must be retained by the board.
– An important decision has to be made to apply for patent protection and accept public disclosure, or not to do so.
– The decision as to which countries the patent should be registered in must be taken carefully. In most cases, patents are applied for only a small number of countries where there is likely to be the technical capability to replicate.
– Inventions made by employees in the normal course of their duties are the property of the employer. In all other cases the invention will be the property

143

of the employee. It is not possible for the employer to contract out of that position. It follows that when first dealing with something which is potentially patentable, it is sensible for the company and the employee to agree at the time who owns the rights and how they are to be exploited.

— The owner of the patent may seek to protect the invention against competitive erosion by continuing to develop new inventions around the original. Such a policy, with its international implications, is an important technical, legal and board matter.

— Any decision to commit a patent infringement must be based on a very careful assessment of the financial consequences. To illustrate the dangers, here is an actual example of a company which took the wrong decision. The company considered that if challenged it had a reasonable defence and it was advised that, even if the challenge was successful, damages would be moderate. (Full accounting provision was made for these.) In the event, the company was charged with infringement and the court decided against it. In assessing damages, the court attached a royalty related not to the value of the small part which was the subject of the patent, but to the whole piece of equipment in which it was assembled and which was in fact highly priced. The damages therefore ran into several hundred thousand pounds and very nearly brought about the company's destruction.

— If it is intended to defend a patent, action should be taken immediately there is knowledge of an infringement. Frequently, an amicable solution can be reached.

— The board should review its patents on a regular basis.

Trade marks

A trade mark is any name or distinctive device warranting goods for sale as the production of an individual or firm.

The intention is that only the owner, or someone licensed by the owner, may lawfully use the trade mark. Registration of trade marks is made at the Trade Marks Registry, thus enhancing the rights of the owner against unauthorised users. Registration can be effected in most other countries. In the UK, the initial registration period is for seven years and may be renewed thereafter for periods of 14 years.

Trade marks are normally used to denote manufacturing origin or trade connections — for example, retail trading signs.

A certification mark relates to types or quality of goods and may be used by any person conforming to the conditions of the mark.

Any trader infringing a trade mark may be guilty of misrepresentation or 'passing off'. Without a registration, however, it may be difficult, time consuming and expensive to prove the point in court under common law procedures.

Designs

It is possible to acquire an exclusive right if artistic effort is applied to a design, which must be new and original, of an industrially produced article. Such a product may be registered with the Registrar of Designs (part of the Patents Office) provided the application is made before the product is released to the public. A manufacturer may clear a new design by filing a request for clearance search with the Design Registry.

Registration gives the right to stop anyone else producing articles which look the same as those of the registered design. The protection is initially for five years with the right to renewal for two further periods each of five years. Infringement may occur whether or not the offending design was intended to copy the registered article: it matters only that it 'looks the same'.

Registered design protection can also be sought internationally.

Copyright

A copyright may be defined as the sole right to reproduce an original literary, artistic, musical or dramatic work. Copyright subsists for a period of 50 years after the author's death. The copyright belongs to the author unless he is an employee, in which case it belongs to the employer. Copyright applies to original computer programs.

Leasehold property

It is almost impossible for a business to trade without the use of property. Most premises are leasehold; freeholds, which in any case are rarely available, lock up substantial amounts of capital which cannot then be effectively employed in the business. However, the occupation of leasehold premises involves entering into significant obligations; a lawyer's advice is essential. The rights and obligations associated with tenancy arise from the terms of the lease and from the Landlord and Tenant Acts 1927 and 1954.

The following points are likely to be covered in any lease:

- the amount of rent payable, provisions for its periodic review and any commencing rent-free period
- the right of the tenant to 'break' the lease and of options to renew at the expiry of the term
- repairing obligations. It is usual to have a 'full repairing and insuring lease'. This imposes on the tenant the full obligation to repair. Therefore, the condition of the premises on entry is very important and a surveyor's report is usually commissioned.
- the conditions governing alterations or improvements to the property
- the right to assign the lease or sub-let the property to some other party (there can be highly restrictive provisions concerning assignment, which will adversely affect marketability). In the case of a sub-let, the tenant will continue to have primary responsibility under the lease with counter rights against the sub-lessee
- restrictions as to user.

Under the 1954 act the tenant has an automatic right to renew his lease provided that:

- the property is comprised in a tenancy
- it is in fact occupied by the tenant
- it is occupied for the purpose of a business carried on by him.

To obtain this protection it is important the procedures set out in the act are precisely followed.

There are grounds under the provisions of the 1954 act upon which the landlord can frustrate the rights of the tenant to a new tenancy: for example, because the tenant has failed to conform with certain material terms of the tenancy, or there has been persistent delay in paying the rent, or the tenant has been offered alternative accommodation. The most likely reason, however, is that the landlord intends to demolish or reconstruct the premises, or that he intends to occupy them for his own purposes; in these events the tenant may seek compensation for disturbance.

There is a growing practice of licensing premises, whereby the owner licenses an occupier for the use of the premises. The provisions of the Landlord and Tenant Act 1954 do not apply to premises which are the subject of a licence.

Insurance

A contract of insurance is between an insurer of the one part who, in consideration of the receipt of a premium paid by the insured of the second part, undertakes to indemnify or compensate him against loss which may occur arising from the occurrence of events specified in the insurance contract.

As with all other contracts, there must be an offer and an acceptance. It is usually the case in insurance that the party seeking insurance initiates the offer through the completion of a proposal addressed to the insurer for his acceptance. Failure on the part of the insured to disclose a material fact in the proposal may result in the refusal on the part of the insurer to pay a claim in due course. It is frequently the practice, therefore, for the proposal to be incorporated into the insurance contract.

Principles of insurance
The principles which underlie all general insurance arrangements are:

- *Insurable interest.* There must be an insurable interest on the part of the insured party which will give rise to a loss resulting from destruction or damage of the thing concerned or give rise to a liability which he must discharge. In the absence of an insurable interest, there can be no insurance.
- *Illegal event.* It is contrary to public policy to arrange insurance against an event which itself is not legal.
- *Utmost good faith.* The insurer must be absolutely truthful in making a proposal to an insurance company. 'Utmost good faith' ('uberrimae fidei') is the essence of the contract between the insured and the insurer. Failure of this principle in relation to material facts or representations will render the policy void. However, some circumstances may be implied and known, or presumed to the known, by the insurer.
- *Indemnity.* An insurance is intended to put the insured who suffers damage and makes a valid claim into the financial position he would have been had the event not occurred. It therefore follows that the insured cannot be in a better position than he would have been had there been no such event. There are, however, some exceptions to the indemnity rule; for example in the case of personal accident insurance.
  There arise two consequences:
  (i) the same risk insured with more than one insurer will still only result in

indemnity. The insurers will contribute to the loss claim pro rata to their share of risk.

(ii) the principle of subrogation comes into force when a claim is settled. In the case of total loss and the insured having been indemnified, any remaining rights and remedies in the insured property after the event are for the benefit of the insurers.

In the case of partial loss, the insurer is subrogated to all the rights and remedies of the insured as from the time of the insured event.

— *Proximate cause.* The event giving rise to a claim must have been caused directly by the risk against which the insurance was taken out.

— *Average.* It is usual for an insurance policy to include an 'average' clause, the effect of which is to indemnify the insured for that proportion of the loss as is represented by the insured value to the total value (the balance being deemed to be self-insured).

Insurance policy is clearly a matter for the board. The implementation of policy may well be assigned by the managing director to the accountant, the company secretary or some other officer (who could be a part-time expert). Apart from establishing policy, the board should always take professional insurance advice and arrange for periodic review of its total insurance cover. This is an area which should always be carefully documented.

Many companies have found it well worthwhile bringing in from time to time a totally independent broker to bid for the insurance business. In this way, gaps in the cover may be exposed, premiums are kept competitive and broker service is maintained at a high level.

It has to be recognised that it is just not possible to insure against all risks. The risks attaching to commercial operations as such are not insurable. And for those risks which are insurable there are always losses which will not be recouped: general disruption to the business causing damage to market share; or the loss of markets, for example, whilst a factory is out of action; and the diversion of top management effort when it turns its attention to the consequences of a major upset. So, while insurance is absolutely necessary, and a great comfort, it is far better that the need to claim does not arise.

It is possible, but not generally recommended, for a company to take a deliberate decision not fully to insure, thus accepting that part of the risk will be taken by the company. For smaller companies this is not an acceptable policy. Larger companies can take a more relaxed view, and in some cases — such as, for example, a retail or hotel chain which can spread the risk — there is a growing tendency to self-insure through a specially set up wholly- or partly-owned insurance company in an overseas tax haven.

Risk assessment

The logical approach is to identify and classify every risk to which the business can be exposed, and systematically to consider and assess each one. This examination will include consideration of the extent to which some of those risk areas can be limited or avoided by alternative commercial arrangements.

The risks should be classified according to their potential effect on the business:

— Risks which go to the root of the whole business. These insurances must be fully covered and always kept under regular review. Very substantial claims for professional negligence, or those arising from product liability (particularly in certain overseas markets) or third party liability arising from explosion or chemical leak make insurance assessment very problematical. If there must be economy in premiums, it is better this takes place in relation to the first layer of cover, with the high risk 'excess' being fully covered.

— *Other risks.* These will be carefully considered for their relative impact on the business. All should, if possible, be fully insured against, but certainly those whose loss or damage will have serious consequences.

Insurance cover

Insurance is needed in respect of both assets and liabilities.

Assets

Full protection must be obtained against damage to or loss of assets important to the operation of the business: there are also risks of damage or loss resulting as a consequence of such an event.

Careful consideration must be given to the possibility of an unusual happening which may not be the proximate cause of the damage typically insured against. Similarly, events which may be quite small in themselves may cause quite disproportionate damage. Or an occurrence elsewhere, not part of the insured's business, may have damaging consequences for that business: for example, a key supplier factory being put out of action for some reason.

Consequential damage should also be fully insured for anticipated net profit, plus ongoing fixed and semi-fixed overheads for a period long enough to put the business back (in so far as that is insurable) into the position in which it was when the loss occurred.

In some cases there is a statutory obligation to insure, for instance, against failure of lifting equipment or power presses, and for related consequential loss.

Liabilities

Third party claims may arise as a consequence of the insured's business activities. Claims can be substantial, arising from defective products or, as has been seen in recent years, chemical explosion.

In the UK there is a statutory requirement to cover with an authorised insurer against motor third party risks and liability to employees for damage suffered arising out of and in the course of their employment.

Data Protection Act 1984

This is referred to in Chapter 9.

Chapter 11

International Trading

The sale or purchase of goods within the UK needs a great deal of care, but trading overseas needs considerably more. Distance, custom, law, taxation, customs duties and language all present additional commercial difficulties.

For these reasons many small to medium-sized businesses fight shy of engaging in overseas trade, particularly exporting. And yet industrial recovery in the UK depends on such companies entering the export market effectively. Moreover, there is in the UK a great deal of practical experience available for, as an island, we have lived by international trade for centuries.

Responsibility again lies with the board. This is where the key decisions must always be taken. There is evidence to show two disconcerting tendencies:

- Boards do not address themselves enough to the policies to be applied to their exporting activities.
- probably arising from this, but not necessarily so, the conduct of sales policies and the physical movement of goods are too often under separate executive control.

Before discussing some of the key aspects of international trading, there are a couple of general points to be made. First, if there is insufficient internal experience, then outside advice must taken. Second, there is no doubt whatever that the ability to communicate in the language of the other party is a great advantage in the conduct of international business. That is irrespective of whether the other party is able to speak English — which he usually can. It is a matter of psychology. It indicates respect for the customer.

The market

It is essential for potential exporters to establish the basic structure of overseas markets and the realistic opportunities for the products to be exported.

This research will not differ in principle from that used in the UK, but it will probably be more expensive and many countries cannot offer the professional competence which can be expected from UK researchers.

The required information will include:

- the political and economic situation, and the probability of stability
- the likely customer need for the product, and pricing constraints
- the amount of adaptation necessary to meet local customer requirements and regulations
- competitive activity, both local and otherwise

- most appropriate distributors, distribution channels and the costs of distribution
- restraints on trade: import restrictions; exchange controls; customs duties
- packaging and design requirements
- translation of publicity manuals and technical instructions
- market pricing structures
- the most effective method of delivery (having regard to customer needs, time and costs)
- local stocking requirements

There are many sources which can be researched to provide data relating to international sales. These include, for example:

- Department of Trade and Industry (different sections deal with, for instance, barter and compensation deals, buying houses, certificates of origin, export licensing and EEC regulations)
- International Chambers of Commerce (particularly as concerns information, customs and practice for documentary credit and market information)
- British Standards Institution
- SITPRO (the simplification of international trade procedures)
- British Overseas Trade Board
- British Export Houses Association
- Institute of Freight Forwarders
- banks (clearing, merchant and foreign)
- trade associations
- foreign embassies in London
- British embassies abroad
- USA (via Commercial Departments of individual states)
- professional firms with an international practice
- Institute of Directors
- British Institute of Management
- Commission of the European Communities
- European Investment Bank
- European Regional Departmental Fund.

The exporter is likely to be dealing with three quite different types of market:

- *Old Commonwealth countries.* In general the practices and laws are often similar to those in the UK and, for historic reasons, will most probably be more familiar to the UK exporter.
- *European.* A growing proportion of UK international trade is with the EEC and non-EEC European territories. Notwithstanding the constantly developing community laws, there are some very real differences between British and European customs and practices. It is very important to have a thorough understanding of the local territorial environment before entering into commercial transactions, and to seek good legal and accountancy advice in connection with the trading methods and structures which should be used.
- *USA.* Deceptively similar on the surface — an impression encouraged by a common language — the USA is in fact a market which is totally different from the UK and should not be attacked without the most thorough preparation. To refer to the USA as a market is itself quite misleading — there are

at least five principal markets comprising the USA, each of which is separate and distinct. At the same time, the whole environment is more encouraging to business, and there are many sources of information willing to assist. Most of the individual states have offices willing and able to assist those intending to locate a business within their jurisdictions. The lawyers are more commercial and accountants are well organised to provide management back-up. If it is decided to establish a place of business in the USA, quality management can almost always be attracted to quite small, or even start-up, operations provided the financial package is right. This will certainly include 'a piece of the action' for senior management. Well over 90 per cent of US companies have fewer than 200 employees, so that establishing a sound operation will not at all be out of context. Of course, the differing state taxation systems will also be a factor to be assessed.

In all cases early consideration should be given to the corporate structure and ownership of any organisation to be permanently located in an export market, and to how the longer-term funding will be approached. If significant losses are anticipated in the early years, it may be wise to structure the company capital to provide some financial protection to the UK holding company; for example, by owning less than 20 per cent of the voting capital to avoid equity accounting. Progressive dilution of ownership may be acceptable to allow for the introduction of tranches of new money to finance a developing business.

Market penetration

There is a choice of several methods by which the UK exporter can try to secure the most favourable market penetration. However, the cost of opening up an overseas market is high, and great caution is required. The exporter may well decide, therefore, to open up the market in phases, to limit the risks and develop distribution as revenues increase.

Sooner or later, the exporter will probably wish to control his own destiny by setting up a sales organisation either of his own or in a joint venture with a national of the country, but it is quite usual to gravitate towards that status, using some agency arrangement in the first place. There are various agencies in this field:

— export merchant	acts as principal
— agent	acts on behalf of the exporter and performs some physical function, but does not take the risk of purchasing and selling the goods
— commission agent	acts on behalf of the overseas buyer, seeking out sources of supply, arranging shipment and finance
— UK buying representative	acts on behalf of overseas buyers on a permanent basis.

Financial assistance, up to 50 per cent of the eligible costs in return for a levy on sales, is available for exporters seeking to open up or expand markets through the Market Entry Guarantee Scheme which is administered by the British Overseas Trade Board.

Regulations

Most goods exported from the UK do not require individual licences, and are covered by an Open General Licence. Information concerning those goods requiring a licence can be obtained from the Export Licensing Branch of the Department of Trade and Industry.

That is unlikely to be the position in the importing country. Restrictions may exist in the form of outright prohibition of specified goods, quota limitations, additional customs duties and tactical frustration of the exporter by rigid and bureaucratic procedures. It is therefore necessary for the exporter to be satisfied that:

- the overseas importer has whatever import permissions are necessary
- there are no payment restrictions preventing the buyer from remitting the amounts due
- he properly understands and conforms with any technical requirements that apply in the import territory.

Although the EEC is intended to be an open common market without restrictions on the movement of goods, in practice this is very far from being the case.

The contract

Export contracts fall principally into the following categories and are covered by the Sale of Goods Act 1979, and the UN convention for the international sale of goods.

- *FOB contracts.* The seller must put the goods free-on-board a ship for despatch to the buyer, although it is normal for the buyer to nominate the port and date of shipment. Once the goods are on the ship, they are normally at the risk of the buyer, who must also pay the freight and insurance charges. Where sea business is involved, the Sale of Goods Act imposes on the seller the obligation to give such notice to the buyer as will enable him to insure the goods during sea passage: failing which they remain at seller's risk, notwithstanding delivery to the carrier.
- *CIF contracts.* If goods are sold at a price which includes the price of the goods, insurance and freight costs to the buyer's destination, it is known as a CIF contract. The time and place of shipment will be treated as conditions of the contract. Risk passes from seller to buyer when the goods are shipped; the property in the goods, however, does not pass until the seller transfers the documents to the buyer and he has made payment in accordance with contract.
- *FAS contracts.* In this contract the seller is required to deliver to the buyer at a named port and to place goods alongside the ship for loading. At that point the property and the risks pass to the buyer.
- *Ex ship.* The seller is responsible for getting the goods to the overseas destination port.
- *Ex works contract.* The buyer takes delivery at the seller's works (or warehouse), and usually property and risk pass at that point.

The sales contract is usually effected by the submission of a 'pro forma' invoice by the exporter and a written acceptance by the importer. This contract determines the precise responsibilities of the parties to the agreement. The principal terms are likely to include:

- *Goods.* Description, quantity, quality specification and packaging.
- *Licences.* The exporter should obtain a copy to satisfy himself that the licence has in fact been issued and to know the conditions to be complied with.
- *Insurance.* It is absolutely essential that there are no mistakes concerning insurance, and that goods are covered throughout the transportation process. The responsibility and risks are determined in the contract.
- *Terms of sale.* These include the arrangements for transportation, delivery and payment, some of which were described above. In fact, only a minority of UK exporters arrange their terms of sale on the basis of a delivered price. Yet the only basis for controlling properly the distribution of the product and its competitive pricing is to sell right into the buyer's market. Boards should always consider trading on the basis of a 'delivered price'.

In international trade it is essential to know the national regulations relating to both exporter and importer, and to observe them to the letter. Otherwise, delays are bound to arise.

Documents

The principal documents required are the invoice, bill of lading and insurance certificate. The invoice should show, in addition to the usual information, details concerning packaging, shipping marks, freight and insurance, import licences and exchange permits. It may also be necessary to provide a certificate of origin and a consular invoice in the importing country.

The bill of lading is the document of title to the goods and therefore provides evidence of their legal ownership. It also serves as a receipt for the goods issued by the shipper to the exporter and of the shipping contract. The bill of lading is a negotiable instrument, and title to the goods passes on endorsement and delivery of the original bill of lading. The shipper will release goods at destination against the original documents which must, therefore, reach the buyer in time to arrange that.

It should be noted that the comparable document for shipment by air, the air waybill, is not a document of title. The consignee can therefore claim the goods once they have cleared customs at the airport of destination.

Payment

This is the crucial issue. The thing to avoid at all costs is any form of court action in a foreign country.

Payment arrangements are affected by the knowledge the parties to the contract have of each other.

The safest way is to receive payment in advance, or at least part payment or a deposit. However, in a competitive situation, it is unlikely that such a method would be acceptable to the importer.

It is more likely that payment will be secured by a confirmed irrevocable documentary letter of credit established in favour of the exporter with a bank in the UK. Again, accurate documentation is vital because banks pay against documents. (*Confirmed:* Putting the obligation on the bank in the UK to make payment

153

irrespective of the buyer's ability to pay. *Irrevocable:* meaning that the obligations cannot be altered except by the agreement of all parties involved.)

Another method of receiving payment is the 'documents-for-collection' basis. All documents are sent via the banks of the two parties. The documents will be released either on payment in cash or against an acceptance — a bill of exchange — which can be payable at sight or over various periods of time as agreed. Such an acceptance can be drawn in sterling on, and accepted by, a UK bank and with this security can be discounted in the money markets.

Trading can also take place on an 'open account' basis. In that case the documents will be sent to the buyer who may pay by cheque or, preferably, by banker's draft or by payment to the exporter's bank by telegraphic transfer. Non-recourse debt collecting can be arranged.

It is sometimes the case that a confirming house acting for the buyer pays for the goods when they are shipped, and carries the risks. The possibility of opening a bank account in the foreign country should also be considered, either to avoid delays in collection or with the intent of using the currency for other transactions in that currency.

Extended credit often plays an important part in negotiating overseas contracts: indeed such terms may be crucial to securing the business. It is essential to discuss the matter with the bank, and the government ECGD facilities are very likely to be used, if available.

In the case of, say, capital equipment it may be possible for the parties to arrange a leasing deal via a finance house. In all such matters expert advice should be taken.

Exchange risks

Careful consideration must be given to the currency in which the goods are invoiced. Although the UK exporter usually thinks of invoicing in sterling, there can be advantage in trading in a foreign currency. Some protection can be obtained by forward dealing in the currency; currency borrowings can be made and repaid in due course from the sale proceeds. Relative interest rates may affect the choice. In all cases expert advice should be taken.

The essential requirement is to limit exchange risk, and this is a matter for the board. The volatility of foreign exchange rates is such that a profitable deal can be turned into a loss if defensive action is not taken. The risks of trading are quite enough already: a trader is not in the business of exchange dealing.

Performance bonds

It is frequently the case that, when bidding for foreign contracts, a tender guarantee and/or performance bond are required as evidence of financial capability to honour the contract. Such guarantees are arranged with the bank and are of course, part of the whole borrowing relationship between the bank and the exporter.

Invisibles

The sale of 'invisible' services on an international basis is just as important as the sale of goods. It may in fact be of more benefit to the UK balance of trade, because it is unlikely to involve any corresponding import of raw materials or partly manu-factured products. The market research necessarily takes a different form from that required for product marketing; and different again from such activities as property development. It should not be assumed that professional services abroad will correspond closely to those available in the UK: there are some quite substantial differences. Take estate agency, for example: there are countries in Europe where it is not unusual for an agent to be also acting as principal in property matters. It is obviously important to appreciate the possibility of that duality: and indeed it may provide a market opportunity to an agency proposing to act professionally in that capacity alone.

The development of international services is a fast growing element in many business areas: particularly in financial and insurance activities, but also in the provision of advertising, marketing, research and promotional services; personnel search, selection and relocation services; and, of course, in travel, tourism hotels and leisure.

Chapter 12

Taxation and the Company

Taxation is a complicated and specialised subject. The board of any company must take expert advice before reaching any decision in which there are taxation implications. And there are not many business decisions where there are not. Morality has very little place in tax matters. The only issue is whether the rules and regulations which have been woven over the years into a web of great complexity are, or are not, complied with.

Tax planning must feature in every company. Every board has a duty to its shareholders to minimise the impact of taxation by organising the business of the company in whatever ways are legally available. It is important to emphasise the matter of legality. Boards can have nothing to do with tax evasion, for that is illegal. What they can and should do is to avoid paying tax which need not be paid. Since form is important in taxation, this is often accomplished simply by arranging a transaction in a different manner, but to the same practical effect.

The application of taxation law to a particular set of circumstances may be unclear to the board. In this case, as in any other where resort to the courts is a possibility, there will be considerable reluctance to pursue matters through legal process unless there are some very important financial issues at stake.

'Not for taxation alone' is a rule which should apply in all business operations. To enter into a transaction whose only real purpose is to reduce tax liability is a very doubtful proposition. In any event, Inland Revenue practice (following the Ramsey and Furness v Dawson court decisions) is to disregard all transactions entered into solely to achieve tax advantage.

This chapter now looks at the various aspects of taxation as it affects companies, first direct taxes and then indirect taxes. UK tax laws apply to companies:

— resident in the UK
— trading in the UK through a branch or agency in respect of profits arising in the UK.

Corporation tax

Tax on companies, known as corporation tax, is charged on the profits of a company according to the rates established in the Finance Acts.

There is special relief for small companies having profits less than £500,000 in the form of a reduced corporation tax rate. The principal conditions are:

— Profits for this purpose comprise those on which corporation tax is paid together with franked investment income (that is, gross income received from a UK resident company, being distributions in respect of which tax credits are granted).

- A reduced rate of tax (30 per cent) is chargeable if the profits of the company do not exceed £100,000.
- For profits between £100,000 and £500,000 there is marginal relief. The tax is then calculated at the full corporation tax rate less a fixed fraction of the amount by which profits fall short of £500,000 (in recent years varying in effect between 3½ and 2¼ per cent).
- Reduced rates as above are levied on a company having no associated companies, ie companies which are either under common control or one controls the other. ('Control' means through voting, or entitlement to the greater part of either the profits or the assets on liquidation. Shares held by husband and wife and minor children are treated as a single holding.)

If there are associated companies, the relevant figures are divided by 1 + the number of associated companies. A group comprising four companies, therefore, will be taxed at the reduced rate in relation to:

£100,000 divided by 4 = £25,000

Marginal relief is applied on the same basis.

Tax rates

Until the Finance Act 1984 the rate of corporation tax was fixed each year for the preceding financial year, ie the year to 31 March. In 1984 there was a change of practice, the rates being fixed for all years from 1983 to 1986 as follows:

Financial year (commencing 1 April)	Full tax rate	Taxable fraction of capital gains
1973-1982	52%	15/26
1983	50%	3/5
1984	45%	2/3
1985	40%	3/4
1986	35%	6/7 (ie effectively 30%)

The imputation system

The company

Since 1973 dividends declared by companies have been paid to shareholders without the deduction of tax. The company must account to the Inland Revenue for tax calculated at three-sevenths of the amount of the dividend, known as Advanced Corporation Tax (ACT). ACT can be deducted from the amount due by the company in respect of its 'main stream' corporation tax.

If however, the company is not liable for any or enough corporation tax on its trading activities to relieve the amount paid by way of ACT on its dividends, there will be a financial burden on the company in respect of the shortfall. This can arise, for example, if a UK holding company is trading substantially through non-UK resident companies. The sort of solution then required is to generate sufficient UK taxable profits to cover the ACT. Such a situation will clearly form part of the tax planning arrangements needing consideration by the directors; in this case, the solution may require, for example, the acquisition of a sufficiently profitable

UK company – provided, of course, it falls within the management skills and competence of the holding company directors.

The individual

A UK company pays dividends of a net amount without deduction of tax. However, the dividend is attributed with a tax credit which effectively amounts to the basic rate of tax – presently 30 per cent. This is the same rate used to calculate the company ACT for which the company must account to the Inland Revenue.

To arrive at the total taxable income of an individual, the tax credit must be added to the net dividend. No further basic rate tax is payable, but the individual may be liable to higher rate tax depending on his total income from all sources. In the event that the individual is not liable for basic rate tax, because his total income is below the basic rate level, there can be no recovery of the tax credit.

Dividends are qualifying distributions. Non-qualifying distributions are distributions of a special nature such as bonus securities carrying a potential future claim on the company's profits. No ACT is payable and the shareholder does not receive a tax credit. Such distributions rank for higher rate tax on the value attributed to them.

Basis of taxation

Corporation tax is charged in respect of accounting periods, which usually coincide with the periods for which the company prepares its accounts, but cannot exceed 12 months (if a greater period, the first 12 months will constitute one accounting period, and the remaining period another). Corporation tax assessments are therefore based on the actual period profits (not those of a preceding year, as is the case with some income tax assessments).

Tax is normally payable nine months after the end of the accounting period or within 30 days of the assessment, if later. If there is a change of tax rate, an accounting period which straddles 31 March will be divided into two parts, each paying the appropriate rate of tax.

Assessable profits

The profits disclosed for the purposes of the company's financial accounts in nearly all cases have to be adjusted for the purposes of arriving at profits for tax purposes. This is because the tax rules differ from the principles adopted for the preparation of financial accounts.

Appendix 17 illustrates some typical adjustments which are likely to be involved in determining profits for tax purposes. Trading profits thus determined are known in taxation terminology as chargeable under Schedule D, case I.

The assessment of income tax is divided by the Inland Revenue into a number of schedules identified by letters of the alphabet. Thus Schedule A covers the income arising from properties. Schedule B profits from woodlands. Schedule D basically deals with trading profits arising from business. There are a number of subdivisions of Schedule D, eg Case I, referred to earlier, assesses trading profits; Case III covers UK interest; Cases IV and V cover income arising from foreign securities and possessions. Schedule E deals with earnings from employment.

The assessments may appear to indicate that some income or profit is escaping tax, but this will not be the case. It will be assessed under some other schedule. This is illustrated at the foot of Appendix 17.

Capital allowances

Capital allowances are given in respect of the purchase cost of certain assets used in the business, such as:

- plant and machinery
- office equipment
- furniture and fittings
- motor vehicles
- industrial, agricultural and forestry buildings
- hotel buildings
- scientific research expenditure
- patents and know-how.

Until 1984, allowances were given equivalent to 100 per cent of the cost of plant and machinery. The Finance Act 1984 changed this practice with the announcement that capital allowances would be reduced to 25 per cent over the ensuing three years. Similarly it was announced that the allowance of 75 per cent for industrial buildings pre-1984 was also to be run down.

Appendix 18 illustrates the type of asset most likely to be encountered in business, and the basis of first-year and subsequent years' 'writing down allowances'.

Arising from the timing differences between the normal method of depreciating assets over their useful lives and the tax system which has encouraged capital expenditure by giving relief during the year of purchase, it is quite normal to find the item 'deferred taxation' shown in the balance sheet as a liability. The directors must form a view as to whether this is an appropriate and reasonable amount based on the probability that the amounts shown will crystallise as actual liabilities as a consequence of the release of deferred tax provisions, and having regard to the rates of tax likely to obtain at the relevant times.

Disposal of assets

Gains and losses are likely to arise when sale proceeds of assets upon which tax relief has been given are compared with the net amount of the asset at that date for tax purposes. If there is a surplus it will be taxed at corporation tax rate as a balancing charge; if a loss, relieved as a balancing allowance.

The sale of certain non-trading assets, eg investments, will give rise to a reduced rate of tax on the surplus realised over cost. If there is a loss, however, it can only be relieved against capital gains tax payable and not against corporation tax. From the table on p158 it will be seen that effectively the appropriate tax rate for such capital gains and losses is 30 per cent.

The treatment of losses

Trading losses can be carried forward indefinitely against the profits of the same trade (but with a limit of six years in the case of losses attributable to stock relief). It may also be noted that losses attributable to first-year capital allowances may be carried back for up to three years. In the case of current trading losses they can alternatively be set off against other profits of any kind for the same, or the preceding, accounting period. Relief is also available against dividends received by the company which are franked, ie have been subjected to a payment of ACT in the hands of the paying company.

It should be noted that the Inland Revenue is likely to apply a very strict definition of 'the same trade'. Take as an example a company which was acquired with substantial unrelieved trading losses. In order to conduct the business in a more profitable manner as part of the acquiring group, the old factory was closed, the sales force reorganised and the management structured into the new group. But the commercial essentials — the product, market-place and customers — were absolutely unchanged. The Revenue sought to contest the relieving of pre-acquisition losses against subsequent profits on the grounds that the company no longer operated 'the same trade'.

Subject to a number of rules, a company making a loss which is part of a group can obtain relief by offsetting that loss against other group companies with taxable profits, including capital profits.

In the case of business termination, a loss in the last 12 months of trading may be carried back against the profits for the three preceding years.

Capital losses may be set off against chargeable gains in the same period. They may also be carried forward to a future accounting period.

Groups of companies

Special provisions relate to UK resident companies which comprise a group; the basic intention of these provisions is to tax the group as though it were a single entity. It works on the following principles:

In respect of not less than 75 per cent ownership of the subsidiary companies:

— Loss relief is available, the effect of which is to offset losses in one company against profits in another or others.
— Transfers of assets within the group do not give rise to capital gains or losses. When the asset leaves the group, capital gains (or loss) will apply, effectively calculated by refererence to its original cost.
— Capital gains tax roll-over relief may be claimed, ie the gain on an asset sold by one company may be set against the purchase price of an asset acquired by another.

In respect of companies owned over 50 per cent:

— Dividend or interest payments from subsidiary to parent may be made free of ACT.
— ACT paid by the parent may be surrendered for relief against a subsidiary company profit.

Close companies

Close companies are those under the control of five or fewer participators or under control of participators (regardless of number) who are directors. For this purpose close relatives count as one and participators include lenders. A UK subsidiary of an overseas parent is close if the overseas parent would have been close if resident in the UK.

A quoted company is not close, provided that at least 35 per cent of the voting shares are held by the public.

The significance of a close company is that the Inland Revenue has the right to apportion to individuals the excess of a company's 'relevant income' over its actual distributions (the definition of distribution is wider than dividends). The purpose of this is to negate accumulations within a family company which may have the effect of avoiding higher rates of personal tax. The rules for arriving at relevant income are complicated, but it should be noted that, since 1980, the trading income of a trading company is excluded from relevant income (ie only investment income is caught). and that distributions are those made during a relevant accounting period, or within a reasonable time thereafter if stipulated as relating thereto, and that loans made by the company to the owners are subject to tax at three-sevenths of the amount, which is charged on the company.

If the loan is 'released' by the company the beneficiary is then subject to higher rate tax.

These provisions, and the rules about cessation of trading and liquidations, are all directed at anti-avoidance arrangements in closely owned companies.

Since 1984 the revenue net has been widened to include UK companies which have interests in controlled foreign companies subject, as might be expected, to a series of complicated rules.

Value added tax

Value added tax (VAT) is levied in effect on the added value arising from the provision of goods or services.

The consequence is that each party in the manufacturing, processing or service chain charges VAT on his 'outputs' or sales and is able to deduct VAT which has been charged on his 'inputs' or purchases. There is a cash flow effect because inputs and outputs arise with each transaction, whereas tax returns are made to Customs and Excise on a quarterly basis. If inputs exceed outputs, there is a tax recovery (and if this happens regularly the taxpayer may elect to account monthly). The practical effect of this is that the company is acting only as agent in the collection process, and does not actually bear any tax. At the end of this attenuated process it is the ultimate purchaser who pays the tax.

There are effectively two rates of tax in the UK: standard VAT (currently 15 per cent) and zero rate. Goods which are classified for zero rating do not carry tax. Under either classification tax which has been incurred on inputs may be recovered.

However, there is another business category — that of 'exemption'. This classification applies mostly to service activities, such as finance and insurance. The practical consequence of this classification is that an exempt company is not able to obtain a full repayment of the VAT suffered on its inputs (depending on the proportion of its exempt to its taxable outputs). These activities therefore constitute an exception to the rule that it is the ultimate consumer who bears the tax.

Registration for VAT is required unless the annual turnover falls below a stated minimum, in which case the trader may elect not be be registered. This means he does not have to charge VAT, nor can he recover VAT suffered.

In the case of a group of companies, the group may elect that one member is treated as the 'representative member' who will be responsible for VAT in respect of the group as a whole. Supplies between group members are disregarded.

Although the principles are straightforward, the practical applications are not. The rules and regulations are complicated, and have to be applied in a technically correct manner. Customs & Excise have wide powers of investigation, and underpayment of VAT can, and usually does, carry a financial penalty. It is therefore important that the board satisfies itself that it has taken good professional advice concerning the implications of VAT in that particular business, the managers receive some instruction about the general principles, and that new systems and methods are reviewed for VAT implications. It may not be generally appreciated, for example, that the recharging of internal services is a VAT event and that input taxes on business gifts (which may include prizes for a sales force) are not allowable deductions. There are many other potential pitfalls, and they can be discovered years after the event took place. VAT planning is therefore essential. Inter alia, VAT 'grouping' must be evaluated: if any of the companies are exempt, or partially exempt, special care is needed.

PAYE

Most people are familiar with the system of tax collection by employer on behalf of the Inland Revenue. An employer has a duty to deduct income tax from an employee's pay whether or not he has been directed so to do by the Inland Revenue. The system applies to all wages, salaries, commissions, bonuses and so on and applies to employees, directors and other office holders. It also applies to pension payments.

Effectively, the PAYE amounts are arrived at by accumulating pay and tax deductions relating to an employee's individual code issued by the Inland Revenue. The amounts so deducted (less tax refunds) during an income tax month must be paid to the Revenue within 14 days of the end of the month, together with deductions in respect of National Insurance.

It may be noted that, under present law, any shortfall in payments due to the Revenue in a winding up can give rise to a personal liability of directors of a company.

Chapter 13

Simple Essentials

This chapter describes a few important aspects of running a business. Some of the points made here are very basic and may seem obvious. But experience has shown that they are not by any means universally understood and put into practice.

Getting your hands dirty

A farmer expects to get dung on his boots — he cannot properly do his job if he doesn't go and see what is actually happening on the farm. The soldier needs his maps and diagrams but knows there is no substitute for inspecting the ground himself. And it is the same in business. Management must be familiar with what is going on in the work areas — there is more flavour in a few minutes spent 'where it's happening' than in all the reports ever written. The manager must keep in contact with reality, and use his eyes and ears.

The telephone

The telephone operator is nearly always the first point of customer contact with a business. First there is the length of time required to have a call answered. That experience — good or bad — will often influence what happens later on; it may affect the mood of the caller before he even starts to discuss business.

Then there is the manner in which the call is answered which could make a strong impression: does the operator seem knowledgable, efficient and courteous? An operator must be trained to the standard required and be well informed about the organisation, being notified as soon as any changes take place.

Next there is the way in which a caller is handled when the person he wishes to speak to is unavailable. Taking down the caller's name, number and, perhaps, the purpose of his call, and then asking him to call back or promising a return call as soon as possible — all this must be done courteously and efficiently. By this time, the caller will have formed some quite definite opinions about the organisation he is dealing with.

It is often the job of the secretary to act as a sort of sieve, protecting her boss from unwanted calls. Indeed, some secretaries create the impression that the boss is unapproachable except by Royalty. On the other hand, some senior and busy people will not have anyone between them and the switchboard; if the call is not wanted, the operator has to react according to whatever directions she has received.

With modern telephone systems, this is a proper use of the operator's time.

Complaints

The handling of customer complaints is the next best indicator of the 'spirit' of a business. The response to the customer is a direct reflection of management attitude. Most people complain only when they feel really aggrieved. For every complaint made, there may well be 99 dissatisfied customers who simply vote with their feet! A high percentage of complaints turn out to be justified.

The handling of complaints should be taken seriously and procedures established. This in fact provides one of the best ways of finding out what is actually going on in your own business. The important principles are first, not to be deflected from getting to the truth of the matter, and second, to make sure that responsibility is accepted by the right person or persons, and not passed on to someone else.

The complaining letter should be acknowledged immediately. If the facts are known, the matter can be dealt with straightaway. If not, confirm that the matter will be investigated and that in due course there will be a further communication. Then get down to having the problem thoroughly investigated until you are absolutely satisfied you have the whole truth. A sensible explanation — or apology — must then be sent to the complainant. There are lessons to be drawn from all complaints, and corrective action may need to be taken. This is not the way things happen in many businesses, which seem to regard complaints as minor irritations to be dealt with as rapidly and quietly as possible, preferably by the complaints department!

Thoroughness is the mark of an effective complaints procedure. The customer almost invariably appreciates the trouble taken and becomes a messenger of goodwill. The organisation learns to adopt a more critical attitude towards its own conduct, which results in improved performance generally. On occasion, it is appropriate for the manager responsible for the problem to visit the customer and to explain matters in person. The customer may be impressed by this attention, and it encourages the manager to take his customer responsibilities seriously.

In any organisation it is quite difficult to find out where things are going wrong. It is worthwhile for complaints to be properly logged — an easy task for a trained secretary. This may show that more can be traced to one area than another.

If the temptation on receipt of a complaint is to send a strong reply of rebuttal, draft it, put it away overnight and think about the reaction of the recipient. In fact, this is not bad advice for other sticky communications as well.

Briefs

Many problems need to be solved by several parties working together. Terms of reference — the brief — must be concise and comprehensive. If the brief is unclear, the report or recommendations are likely to be faulty.

The manager must give considerable thought to the problems to be examined, and he should take responsibility for signing off the terms of reference, even if others have taken part in their drafting. Preparing good briefs is not that easy, and the opinion of colleagues is valuable in pointing out the weak points. The brief should, of course, finish up with a clear statement as to what is required.

It is also sensible to discuss the brief with the person who will have responsibility for responding to it. Any possible areas of misunderstanding should be eliminated before any work is done. If the study is complex it is valuable to have a number of points during the course of the work, at which the parties undertake a verbal review, or produce an interim report. This ensures that the response remains consistent with the interpretation of the brief.

Aide-mémoires and minutes

There is no substitute for making a quick note about a meeting as soon as possible after it is concluded. The memory gets blurred after a few days, especially if events are moving rapidly. A note made immediately means that the facts and atmosphere are likely to be more accurately recorded.

Minutes of meetings should also be dictated — or written — quickly after the meeting. Minutes should seldom be a verbatim record of the discussion. They are a summary. Summarising and recording accurately requires a certain skill, and it is certainly made easier if it is done soon after the meeting.

Notes of all kinds must be made bearing in mind all those who may be affected — not necessarily the same people who attended the meeting. Sufficient consideration is often not given to who 'needs to know'. The distribution list is usually openly recorded but, particularly in the case of correspondence, there will be occasions when some recipients are best not shown openly.

Correspondence

This is another way in which an organisation shows its character. Correspondence should be responded to promptly, even if this is only by way of an acknowledgement in the first instance. This applies to both internal and external communications, although within the organisation a telephone acknowledgement may be sufficient. Ignoring correspondence or only responding to it after a delay is discourteous and bad for morale. Dealing effectively with correspondence should be a routine discipline of the office. Either a reply is sent giving the answer straightaway, or a holding reply sent pending further information. In the latter case, as with all incomplete business, it gets put into a 'bring forward' system. And that's where it stays, review after review, until the correspondence is properly closed.

Honouring undertakings

When you say you will do something, then do it. If you say 'I will ring you back', then do it as soon as you are able. Or send a message saying why you cannot and when you will. If you say you will deliver something by a certain date, do so. Do not start to think that a couple of days won't matter if it turns out to be inconvenient to deliver as promised. Delays and postponements are often unnecessary. Of course, it is better to agree a date than to impose one. But if you do receive what appear to be unreasonable instructions to deliver something by a date, it is often worthwhile trying to do it, even if it means working all night!

There is one type of transaction in which it is fatal not to honour dates — and that is a financial transaction. If you have arranged a repayment programme with your bankers, stick to it — even if you have to re-borrow immediately in order to do so! If events are clearly changing for the worse, give plenty of warning and frequent information. No manager, or banker, or board welcomes surprises.

If there is bad news ahead, prepare people for it as well as you can. Good news is different, people don't need warning of this.

Praise where praise is due

It is important for a manager to offer praise when things are done well. People respond to a little encouragement; they will do all sorts of things to help when you need it and they will accept fair criticism on other occasions. There is nothing more demotivating than being ignored, not knowing whether your boss thinks you have done something well or badly. It is not very difficult to congratulate or to thank somebody, but it is a rare manager who gives enough thought to this side of his work.

Chapter 14

The International Challenge

Movements in the international currency markets are as good an indicator as there can be of the relative competitive positions of the major trading countries. The efficient operators – the US, Germany and Japan in particular – have enjoyed continuously strengthening currencies. The UK has not.

Figure 14.1 illustrates the sad story of UK commercial performance in dollar terms since the last war. Indeed, decline had been continuous for the half century before then. Figure 14.2 shows the relative position of sterling compared with a basket of other currencies since 1975. This is no more comforting, especially as it includes the benefits of North Sea oil.

In terms of world trade, the UK has registered a continuous decline in market share. At the turn of the century the UK held about one-third of it. This had dropped to about one-fifth in the 1950s, and is currently around 7 per cent. Japan's share of world trade has steadily increased to about one-fifth at the present time. The unit cost of UK manufactured goods in real terms is higher now than 10 years ago, nearly all attributable to increased labour costs.

Between 1981 and 1985 sterling fell by 22 per cent against the US dollar (having nearly touched par at one point early in 1985) and 14 per cent against a basket of currencies. Although exports since 1980 have increased in sterling terms, imports have outpaced them. The consequence of this trade deterioration is a swing on

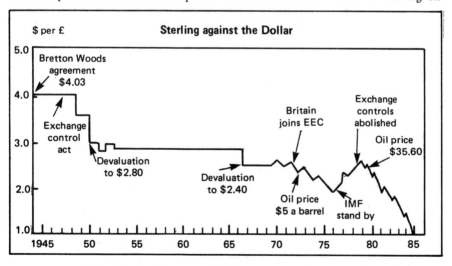

Figure 14.1. *Sterling measured against the US dollar 1945-1985*

visible trade account from a surplus in 1980 of almost £1 billion, with oil neutral, to a deficit in 1984 of around £4 billion, with oil contributing £7 billion. Fortunately for the UK, invisibles just about neutralised the external account in that year.

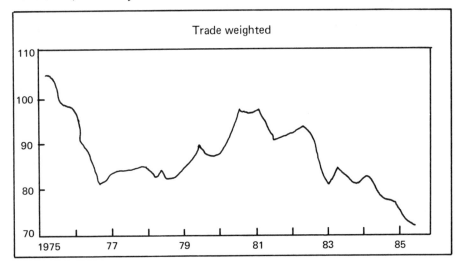

Figure 14.2. *Trade weighted sterling index*

All of us seek improved standards of living and better public services — health, education, infrastructure and environment. What has not been sufficiently accepted in the UK is that resources can only be made available for those desirable purposes from the earnings of UK industry, commercial and financial services. They are not there by any right and they cannot be legislated for. Nor can they be made available by use of the government printing press, nor by paying ourselves more than the real growth in national productivity. They can be secured only as a result of winning more business from determined professional competitors.

The Times Financial and Industry section in February 1985 stated:

> *A sample comparison between British and German metal bashing plants in the latest National Institute Economic Review reveals that the productivity of German workers is 60 per cent higher than that of the British. It is, after all, higher productivity that allows a higher standard of living, even if that transparent truth is frequently ignored.*
>
> *The question is, why?*
>
> *. . . As anyone who has looked for five minutes at the Japanese or German approach to things would identify, the basic difference comes in attention to detail in the (mainly small to medium-sized) German firms studied. . .*
>
> *The National Institute focused on the lack of technical skill and training, from the top to the bottom of the firms. . . . The gap between the technical expertise and formal qualifications of foremen and supervisors in the two countries was particularly glaring.*

The UK starts with many benefits: accumulated capital from the past, an almost unique geographical position, considerable natural energy resources, a stable political environment and an intelligent people. What we have failed to do is sufficiently to harness these enviable attributes into an effective competitive business community. Of course, there are many outstanding exceptions to this general uncompetitiveness, but they represent too small a proportion of the national productive capacity.

Because the vast majority of wealth producing capability is represented by small and medium-sized businesses, it follows that it is from these companies that progress must come.

And that means from improved management. It is a fact that we, as a nation, have handicapped ourselves by a trade union structure which has too much power, too narrow a vision and is insufficiently accountable for its actions. This has restricted essential change and pushed wages up to the detriment of unit output costs which compare badly with those of our international competitors. While some legislative steps are now being taken to bring about changes in the status of trade unionism, the main impetus simply has to come from a more enlightened workforce and an improved performance by managers.

If this book, addressed to the managers of small and medium-sized businesses and their advisers, can in any way assist that challenging process, it will most certainly have served its purpose.

Appendices

Appendix 1

Shareholders' Capital

ORDINARY SHARES

Can be *voting* or *non-voting*. The practice of issuing non-voting shares is, today, not well regarded. If there are non-voting shares they will have all the rights and obligations of voting shares with the important exception that they have no say in the conduct of the company. Voting ordinary shares ultimately control the destiny of the company: appoint the directors; control changes in the company constitution; and assume the 'end' financing risk.

PREFERENCE SHARES

Can be:

(a) redeemable
(b) non-redeemable
(c) cumulative as to dividend

or, less frequently:

(d) can participate in profits

Company law and the Memorandum and Articles of Association will define their rights.

In essence, however, a preference share normally carries a fixed dividend which accumulates if not paid. It will rank in priority over ordinary shares for payment of the preference dividend and in return of capital in a winding-up.

It is often the case that voting rights attach to preference shares if the dividend is in arrear for more than a stated time.

To protect the capital of the company, the redemption of preference shares can only take place either from accumulated profits available for distribution or from the proceeds of a fresh issue of shares made for the purpose.

DEFERRED SHARES

Fairly unusual. They may arise from a reorganisation of capital and be relatively valueless. Or they may have residual rights standing after preference and ordinary shares. Almost invariably non-voting.

Appendix 2

Statement of Source and Application of Funds

for the (period) ended _____ 198-

	£
Source of Funds	
Profit on ordinary activities before tax	750.000
Adjustment for items not involving the movement of funds	
— depreciation	50.000
— goodwill	10.000
— profit on sale of tangible fixed assets	(5.000)
Funds generated from operations	805.000
Other sources:	
— sale of tangible fixed assets	20.000
— term loan from XYZ Bank	75.000
Total funds generated	900.000
Application of Funds	
— purchase of fixed tangible assets	25.000
— repayment of medium-term loan	300.000
— dividend paid	120.000
— taxation paid	130.000
	575.000
Increase in Working Capital (as below)	325.000
Total funds applied	900.000
Movements in Working Capital	
— increase in stock and work in progress	250.000
— increase in debtors	200.000
— (increase) in creditors	(100.000)
Movement in Net Liquid Funds	350.000
— (decrease) in bank balances	(25.000)
	325.000

Appendix 3

Financial Ratios

Part I

Example of operating ratios

Ratio	Purpose	Method
1. Gross margin	Shows gross profit in relation to net sales revenue. A business must establish a high gross margin to generate satisfactory net profits (provided the end result of optimum gross profit is achieved).	$\dfrac{\text{Gross profit}}{\text{Net sales}}$
2. Net profit margin	To establish the net profit in the business as the source of shareholder returns and retention for development	$\dfrac{\text{Net operating profit}}{\text{Net sales}}$
3. Operating asset turnover (efficiency ratio)	To establish the rate at which net assets employed in operations are being turned over	$\dfrac{\text{Net sales}}{\text{Net operating assets}}$
4. Stock turnover	To establish the number of times inventories are sold and replaced	$\dfrac{\text{Cost of goods sold}}{\text{Average stock level}}$
5. Stock cover in days	To establish the estimated number of days sales cover in stock	$\dfrac{\text{Average stock level}}{\text{Average daily cost of goods sold (as estimated for future periods)}}$
6. Current ratio	Basic test of the ability to meet current obligations. A key to solvency.	$\dfrac{\text{Current assets}}{\text{Current liabilities}}$

Ratio	Purpose	Method
7. Acid test	Establishes the ability to pay short-term liabilities without having to realise inventory	$$\frac{\text{Cash and marketable securities and accounts receivable}}{\text{Current liabilities}}$$
8. Gearing ratio	To establish the extent of risk arising from the level of borrowings	$$\frac{\text{Borrowings}}{\text{Shareholders funds}}$$
9. Average debt collection period	To establish the number of days credit being granted	$$\frac{\text{Average accounts receivable}}{\text{Average daily sales}}$$
10. Average trade credit period	To establish the number of days credit being taken from suppliers	$$\frac{\text{Average accounts payable}}{\text{Average daily purchases}}$$
11. Employee performance	To establish employee productivity	a) $$\frac{\text{Net sales revenue}}{\text{Average employment headcount}}$$ b) $$\frac{\text{Net profit}}{\text{Average employment headcount}}$$ c) $$\frac{\text{Employment costs}}{\text{Value added}}$$

Part II

ICC business ratios (see note)

STANDARD INDUSTRIAL CLASSIFICATION 6410 – FOOD RETAILING

	1984	1983	1982	1981	1980	1979
Financial Ratios						
Return on capital employed %	27.8	21.0	21.2	21.2	22.9	27.6
Profit margin %	3.1	2.4	2.7	2.4	3.1	3.1
Liquidity (current ratio)	1.3	1.2	1.2	1.4	1.4	1.2
Stock turnover (days)	23.9	26.5	26.8	25.3	17.2	16.4
Gearing	0.1	0.1	0.1	0.1	0.1	0.1
Employee based (£000)						
Sales per employee	62.2	58.7	56.8	45.3	44.2	31.9
Profit per employee	1.32	1.27	1.01	0.87	0.98	0.82
Fixed assets per employee	7.9	7.3	6.6	5.5	5.8	3.7
Average renumeration	4.6	4.56	4.26	3.50	3.13	2.63

Note: Figures shown are for upper quartile companies.
Source: ICC Database (February 1986)

Note re discounted cash flow

The purpose of this calculation is to recognise the effects of timing on cash movements. A pound today obviously does not have the same value in, say, 10 years time, even assuming nil inflation, because of the interest factor.

The technique can basically be used to provide information in two different ways.

Net present value

The first is to apply a certain interest rate to a future flow of cash movements of which the payment dates are known or assumed. Discounting each cash movement back to the present time gives a 'net present value' and can be useful in comparing alternative possibilities.

Internal rate of return

The second way is to calculate what rate of interest is necessary to discount a future payment to a present value of nil. This provides the 'internal rate of return' which can be used for comparative purposes. For example, this technique has been used to calculate the rate of return on a venture capital portfolio invested and realised over a period of years, thus providing a guide to the value of putting resources into that activity as compared with alternative possibilities.

Appendix 4

Bringing a New Product to Market

Note: It is assumed that there is enough knowledge to have identified the marketing opportunity for a specific type of product.

Objective

The company's objective in this proposed product area should be carefully defined. This might be stated as:

'To become the market leader in the UK (product) market within the next five years.'

1. *Initial product identification*

   (a) definition of possible products and associated benefits
   (b) production of prototypes for use in market research and for technical testing.

2. *Market research* (including in-house knowledge)
   Define:

   (a) the required product benefits
   (b) target consumer profile
   (c) pricing
   (d) packaging
   (e) other product attributes, eg sizes, colours, etc.

   Note: *The research may include professionally constructed consumer panels (ie small groups of individuals, brought together to discuss the product merits under the guidance of professional researchers).*

3. *Commercial feasibility*
   Evaluate:

   (a) estimated market and potential market share
   (b) product margins
   (c) investment required:
       (i) capital
       (ii) marketing
   (d) return on investment required.

4. *Decision to proceed*

5. *Product development*
   (a) development of chosen product and thorough product testing against identified product requirements
   (b) re-examination of product design to reduce production costs (engineers to 'design out' costs)
   (c) definition of tooling and costs
   (d) definition of production requirements, factory usage and related costs
   (e) production planning
   (f) production testing.

6. *Marketing plans*
   (a) product positioning
   (b) product benefits
   (c) target customer groups
   (d) target distribution channels
   (e) pricing policy
   (f) practical testing of packaging.

7. *Communications plans* – internal and external

8. *Implement*
   (a) packaging
   (b) advertising
   (c) public relations
   (d) sales literature
   (e) point of sale.

9. *Organise sales force*

   Detailed sales targets:
      (i) phased;
      (ii) defined by class of trade, major customer etc.

10. *Prepare launch*
    Preparation and implementation of detailed promotion plans, to include launch plans for consumer and the trade.

11. *Sales launch*
    Briefing of the sales force:
    (a) product benefits
    (b) sales policy
    (c) pricing and discount policy
    (d) sales quotas and incentives.

Appendix 5

A Business Plan Framework

1. *Business mission:* A statement of the business which the company perceives itself to be in and its intentions in that chosen field.

2. *Background:* A statement of recent history and current involvement.

3. *Corporate objectives*
    - business development and growth
    - financial
    - quality criteria
    - employee participation and motivation
    - communications
    - exit.

4. *Marketing plan*
    - market research and analysis
        - market size composition and trends
        - competition
        - market share and position
        - future market development
    - market strategy
    - product positioning
    - pricing policies and margins
    - servicing policy
    - advertising and promotion
    - design
    - communications.

5. *Product plan*
    - identification of opportunities
    - protection
    - product innovation and development.

6. *Sales plan*
    - order intake and backlog
    - margins
    - price and discount policy

182

- introductory offers
- sales force
- remuneration
- advertising and PR
- communication
- after-sales service.

7. *Operations plan*

- product development
- product sourcing
- quality criteria
- product, operating and unit costs
- operating standards
- research.

8. *Manpower plan*

- planned requirements
  - categories
  - qualities
  - skills
- selection and recruitment
- training and development
- industrial relations and communications
- pay and benefits.

9. *Technical plan*

- technical intelligence
- developing technical solutions
- system specifications
- space requirements
- initiate technical proposals.

10. *Organisation and control plan*

- projection of requirements
- organisation plan
- communications.

11. *Financial plan*

- profit and loss accounts
- balance sheets
- cash flows
- funding requirements and plans
  - short
  - medium
  - long
- reports.

12. *Communications plan*
    - external
      - trading
      - customers
      - intelligence
      - markets
    - internal
      - operational
      - philosophy
      - financial
      - control
      - personnel
    - design
    - audio and visual aids
    - electronic communications.

13. *Risk analysis and contingency plan*
    - order intake
    - margins
    - fixed costs
    - liquidity.

14. *Action plan*

Appendix 6

A Business Plan for a Small Company

Free Publications Limited

CORPORATE PLAN 1983-87

Index

Note: All figures shown are hypothetical.

1. Background

Free Publications commenced trading in June 1976 with a share capital of £970 and an overdraft facility of £100,000. The share capital was increased to £80,000 in 1980. On occasions, it has been necessary to seek additional temporary bank facility, but basically the company has managed its cash flow within the original facility. At the end of 1982 the company publishes eight magazines involving the issue of 7.5 million copies in 1982-83 and if continued, 9.3 million copies in 1983-84.

The financial history of the company is set out in Appendix B, together with a note of some significant factors affecting the results, including exceptional items. A comparison with respective budgets indicates a trading optimism in their preparation, although economic conditions have also deteriorated during the periods covered. The incidence of profits is unusual. The bunching of autumn publications very significantly affects the last financial quarter results. This pattern has meant that cash flows are not cumulatively positive until the closing months.

2. Corporate objectives

(i) To continue to hold the position as recognised leader in the business of high

quality specialised magazines distributed by methods not involving significant sale to the public through traditional outlets and which either:

(a) depend wholly or substantially on advertising revenue as the source of income or
(b) depend on fee income in respect of arranging the publication or payment by a single sponsor.

Although in practice difficult to achieve, the company aims for improved security and profitability through participation in cover sales.
(ii) To develop other business activities either related to and arising from the existing magazines (line extensions) or from the skills of the company in relation to other publishing activities (such as information booklets).
(iii) To aim for pre-tax profits based on the following criteria:

(a) revenues growing at approximately 25 per cent from an assumed base in 1982-83 of £2m
(b) profits before tax representing 10 per cent of net revenues in 1982-83 and rising by equal amounts to 15 per cent in 1987.

The targets therefore are:

£000 (in 1982 currency)

	Net revenues	Net profits	
1982-83	2,000	10%	200
1983-84	2,500	11.25%	280
1984-85	3,000	12.5%	375
1985-86	3,750	13.75%	515
1986-87	4,500	15%	675

(iv) To achieve these objectives without recourse to a banking facility in excess of £100,000 and to aim to have no recourse to banking finance from 1984-85.
(v) To structure the company in such a manner that it will have the management resources to provide the capability of continuing in its own progression, being attractive to a purchaser or an appropriate vehicle for an Unlisted Stock Market quotation.
(vi) To study other business opportunities as they may arise and within the competence of the company skills. Because of the need to concentrate on the principal mainstream activities of the company, the pursuit of this objective is conditional upon:

(a) the management being able to devote the necessary time to the project without material damage to existing activities;
(b) the managing director obtaining board approval of the project at an early stage in the investigation and its resource implications.

3. Factors affecting the achievement of the objectives

(i) *Objectives 1 and 2*
(a) The company believes that the strength attaching to the existing business lies in the fact that it has considerable know-how and experience in the

publication of magazines directed at a specific consumer market, dependent wholly or substantially on advertising revenues and requiring close client involvement.

Publication E departs from this formula in the sense that it does not have as much security from its clients' business as is the usual case, and must compete more openly with publications aimed at the same market sector.

(b) The perceived success of the company has resulted in competitors observing the formula and attempting imitation.

A note on the presently known competition situation is shown in Appendix C. The company therefore believes that development of the existing formula remains very important in order to protect the company's business and make it more difficult for competitors to enter significant market sectors.

Identification of clients representing the best in their field is important for the company to maintain its market leadership.

(c) A problem exists from restrictive covenants in existing clients' contracts which prevent the company entering the market with others in the same field. This imposes some restriction on future business development and efforts should be made where possible to avoid contract constraints.

(d) The company should, nevertheless, conduct its operations on the basis that there is a strong competitive threat, and therefore must be able to see fairly clearly the outline of the development of the business over the next two to three years;

(e) The company must exploit fully each publication by pursuing line extensions in order to achieve maximum profits, maintain itself as market leader and, very importantly, cement close client relationships.

(f) The success of some publications turns on close involvement by the company with the client. Absence of this ingredient is usually fatal.

(ii) *Objective 3*

(a) It is assumed that within the existing formula it should be possible for the company to develop new product applications where the contributions are likely to grow at a more rapid rate than the central overhead. This has not so far been the case, but it is important that overheads assume a decreasing proportion of revenue if the net profit targets are to be achieved.

(b) Each individual magazine product should:

● contribute a minimum 15 per cent of net advertising revenue at the contribution stage and definitely aim for 25 per cent. For the purposes of the financial model (see paragraph 4) the overall contribution for 1982-83 is assumed at 20 per cent, improving each subsequent year by 0.5 per cent.

● Each issue should on average through the year contribute a minimum of £15,000.

Qualifications:

● There may be 'one-off' opportunities of an exceptional nature which

187

should be considered on their merits.

- Experience has shown that there is a fairly long build up period — perhaps up to two years after the first issue.
- Current economic conditions militate against optimum profitability. The commonsense view must be that the planned targets may not be currently possible with all products, provided it is calculated that they will be on return to more 'normal' market conditions.

(c) We are making the assumption that, due to growth, we can expect a more favourable central overhead cost as we move forward from our current 1982-83 base.

We therefore plan for a consistent reduction in the proportions the general overhead costs bear to net revenues as follows:

	% of net revenues
1982-83	10
1983-84	9
1984-85	8
1985-86	7
1986-87	6

'Overheads' are here defined as those costs which cannot properly be attributed to selling, editorial and print costs (including printing control).

(iii) *Objective 4*

Achievement of this objective will be considerably helped by smoothing of the spring and autumn peaks. This can be achieved by any, or a combination of all, of:

(a) developing products whose publication dates differ from that traditional spend period;
(b) developing products with more frequent issue basis.

It is important to the good health of the company that we find a satisfactory method of smoothing profits and cash flows (and thus avoid the year end miracle).

(iv) *Objective 5*

The build-up of competent key management is the most important investment the company will make. Care, however, should be taken not to overstaff, and the use of freelance services should always be considered when appropriate. The company cannot afford to carry excess staff or nonperformers.

There should be a constant search for quality performance and frankness in rating personal assessments.

(v) *Objective 6*

We feel that the development of an alternative profit area will be most easily and probably more professionally achieved if we are able to adapt what we know into new areas. Otherwise it will mean recruiting a whole new range of management skills and moving into rather uncharted areas, making the risk greater. This has been our experience so far. On the other hand, our options must be kept open for outstanding opportunities. We feel that this type of activity should preferably be undertaken through a subsidiary company in order to protect the main business. Our shortcomings outside the publishing business should, however, be recognised. Self-discipline is required, and proper regard paid to the conditions set out in the objective.

4. Business model

Based on the data previously established, the business model may be summarised during the period as follows:

1983 £000

		1982-83	1983-84	1984-85	1985-86	1986-87
Net revenues		2,000	2,500	3,000	3,750	4,500
Contribution	%	20	20.5	21	21.5	22
	£	400	512	630	806	990
General overhead		200	225	240	262	270
	%	10	9	8	7	6
Net profit	£	200	287	390	544	720
	%	10	11.45	13	14.5	16
Plan target	%	10	11.25	12.5	13.75	15

Restated assumptions

Contribution	Rising by 0.5 per cent from a base of 20 per cent. This is very important to profitability as the benefit moves directly to net profit.
Overheads	Reducing by 1 per cent from a base of 10 per cent.

5. 1982-83

The budget discloses the following:

(a)	Issues	Av contrib per issue	% Mag revenue	% Total revenue	Budget £000	% Total revenue
Total revenue					2,175	100
Contributions						
Publication A	4	16.5	20.0	14.4	66	
Publication B	4	20.0	22.0	17.5	80	
Publication C	4	12.2	23.4	10.7	49	
Publication D	2	10.0	18.0	4.4	20	
Publication E	4	12.0	19.0	10.5	48	
Publication F	4	15.0	17.0	13.1	60	
Publication G	2	10.0	15.0	4.4	20	
Publication H	4	18.5	14.5	16.2	74	
Other				8.8	40	
				100.0	457	21
Overhead					(170)	7.7
Management profit, pre tax					287	13.3

Management profit, pre tax	287	13.3
Board contingency	(136)	(6.3)
Budget profit, pre tax	151	7

(b) *Comparison with corporate objectives*

	Model	% Revenue	1982-83 Budget	% Revenue
Revenue	2,000		2,175	
Contributions	400	20	457	21
Overhead	(200)	(10)	(170)	(7.7)
Contingency	–	–	(136)	(6.3)
Net profit	200	10	151	7

6. Product development

The following are currently under consideration:

(i) *Magazine*
   (a) Publication J
   (b) Publication K
(ii) *Line extensions*
   Publication C – direct response proposals.

7. Negative decisions

It would be helpful if the company were more exactly to define its market sector by determining what it does not intend to do. This includes:

(i) not moving into areas for which it does not presently have the skills and experience;
(ii) not moving into publications primarily dependent upon the servicing by news agency distribution channels;
(iii) not moving into areas likely to be damaging to the company corporate image now being established by the publication of high quality magazines.
   Subsidiary Ltd can be used for non-magazine purposes but even then care must be taken.

8. Short-term action plan

	Action	Progress review
1. All senior management to search consistently for product line extensions	All management	3 months
2. Establish characteristics and identify six brand targets	MD	Feb board
3. Identify significant market sectors, target clients for application of existing magazine formula	MD	6 months

	Action	*Progress review*
4. Seek monthly (say 10 a year in practice) publication or single annual issue in December to smooth business flow. *NB.* Could include a professional publication	Non-executive director	3 months
5. Circulate publication K and arrange Acorn presentation	MD	1 month
6. Improve agency contact and information about company activities	Lunch-room proposal	Immediate
7. More diverse printing arrangements to avoid dependence on single supplier.	Executive director	Continuous

9. Review of last year's plan

How well did we do against the objectives we had set ourselves at the beginning of the year?

(a) *Profits*

Due to the continued recession the level of revenue budgeted was not obtained.

	Budget	*(%)*	*Actual*	*(%)*
Revenue				
Publication A	308		258	
Publication B	336		296	
Publication C	160		196	
Publication D	127		140	
Publication E	176		142	
Publication F	268		205	
Publication G	271		170	
Other	75		85	
	1,721	100	1,492	100
Contributions				
Publication A	68		52	
Publication B	66		55	
Publication C	24		48	
Publication D	32		36	
Publication E	38		36	
Publication F	58		30	
Publication G	54		33	
Other	20		5	
	360	20.9	295	19.7
Overhead	173	10.0	249	16.7
Profit	187	10.9	46	3.0

(b) *Action plan*

1. During the year the team was strengthened by employing an editor-in-chief as planned.
2. Line extensions continued to be sought and a further edition of the ( ) related to publication C was produced.

Appendix A: Publications

Title	Frequency	Issues 1982-83	Copies 1982-83 000	Copies 1983-84 000
Publication A	Quarterly	4	1,000	1,000
Publication B	Quarterly	4	800	1,000
Publication C	Quarterly	4	800	1,000
Publication D	Bi-annually	2	500	500
Publication E	Quarterly	4	1,400	2,000
Publication F	Quarterly	3	1,400	1,800
Publication G	Bi-annually	2	600	800
Publication H	Quarterly	4	1,000	1,200
Total			7,500	9,300

Appendix B: Financial summary from 1979

Years ending December:

	1979 1980 1981 1982	Budget management target 1983 £000	Plan 1983 £000
1. Revenues		2,175	2,000
2. Contributions £	Details omitted	457	400
%		21.0	20
3. General overhead £		170	200
%		7.8	10
4. Net trading £		287	200
% of rev		13.2	10
% of contribs		62.8	50
5. Bank interest		–	–
6. Exceptional items/ contingency (Notes A–E refer.)		136	–
7. Net budget profit before tax		151	200

Notes
A. Twelve months' sales expenses against first three issues.
B. Investment in an associated company written off in full.
C. Claim for loss of profits on breach of contract.
D. Including bad debt provision.
E. Not including development costs in subsidiary.

Appendix C: The competition
(First part only for illustration purposes.)

The market has exploded and further growth seems assured. We believe that *proving claims via research coupled to absolute respectability* − wins all. This is true for newspapers and magazines.

We only need to concern ourselves with magazines because almost all free newspapers rely on local advertisers for their revenue. There is no clash of interest.

The magazine market should be divided into three:

(i) Trade
(ii) Non-conflicting consumer
(iii) Conflicting consumer.

The first major problem is that it is next to impossible to find out the true state of the market. Nobody keeps any accurate data. The nearest is *BRAD*. Not all titles (by far) are listed. None has a guaranteed circulation figure. They are not categorised together and it is very difficult to distinguish at a glance who does what.

We think it fair to ignore our first category. We do not publish any trade magazines and the revenue they earn does not in any form conflict with us.

Example of Company Objectives/Action Plan

Annual Plan 198-

Note: Ca = Continuous action
* = Months before

Objective	Who responsible	By when	Basis of measurement
1. *Set key objectives*	A	Q1-3*	Document
2. *Marketing*	B		
(a) Verify list prices and agreements are consistent with gross margin objectives		Q1-1*	Report
(b) Develop medium-term advertising and PR plan		Q3	Plan
(c) Define marketing plans for:			
(i) local government		Q2	Plan
(ii) financial sector		Q3	Plan
(d) Define and plan specialist product markets		Q1	Plan
(e) Develop a strategic plan for product X		Q4	Plan
(f) Define market requirements for product Y line extensions		Q3	Proposal
(g) Establish contracts in three international markets	D	Q4	Contracts
3. *Key management*	A		
(a) Find and appoint new marketing director		Q3	Appointment
(b) Find and appoint finance director		Q2	Appointment
(c) Find and appoint sales manager for government accounts		Q2	Appointment
(d) find and appoint technical director		Q4	Appointment
(e) find and appoint manager for information systems		Q3	Appointment

Objective	Who responsible	By when	Basis of measurement
4. Sales	C		
(a) Achieve orders, revenues and backlog per budget		Ca	Management Accounts
(b) Achieve gross margins per budget			
(i) all products			Management accounts
(ii) service			Management accounts
(c) Penetrate the sector market with product Z per agreed target by achieving £ sales			Management accounts
(d) Achieve additional sector contracts with product A			Management accounts
(e) Continue the development of the XYZ account to build a sound base for future business			Report and accounts
(f) Make substantial progress by increasing sales to local government			Management accounts
(g) Make substantial progress by increasing sales to the financial sector			Management accounts
(h) Open new accounts with Product X			Sales reports
5. Product development	E		
(a) Complete market introduction of new model of product T		EndQ3	Plan and product release
(b) Complete integration of products S and V		Q2	Report
(c) Determine implementation plan for product X line extension		Q2	Plan
(d) Improve quality of product Y		Q4	Demonstrate
(e) Redesign product W to show cost reduction of 20 per cent		Q3	Cost report
6. Manufacturing	F		
(a) Improve delivery achievement to better than 90 per cent		Ca	Monthly reports

Objective	Who responsible	By when	Basis of measurement
(b) Improve quality performance throughout		Ca	— Quality reports
			— Customer analysis
			— Subcontractors' delivery reports
(c) Achieve or better inventory levels		Ca	Management accounts
(d) Introduce product T to achieve customer deliveries this year		Q4	
7. *Customer service*	G		
(a) Increase range of services and prepare sales plan for them		Q3	Report and plan
(b) Significantly reduce customer complaints		Ca	Complaints log and reports
8. *Information systems* Analyse, review and recommend action in priority order	H	Q4	Report
9. *Financial*	All		
(a) Achieve or better budget in all areas		Ca	Management accounts
(b) Improve cash flows by: (i) reducing debtors to 55 days	J	Ca	Management accounts
(ii) reducing inventories without loss of efficiency to 95 per cent of budget		Ca	Management accounts
(c) Improve NOA turn from plan 2.5 to 3.0.		By Q4	Management accounts
10. *International* Review the company position in the USA and recommend revised strategy	A/D	By Q2	Report

Appendix 8

Date:

F = Forecast
A = Actual

Rolling Six-months Cash Flow Forecast

(Revised monthly)

For January 198-

Period		Week 1		Week 2		Week 3		Week 4		Feb	Mar	Apr	May	June	Total 6 mos
		F	A	F	A	F	A	F	A	F	F	F	F	F	F
RECEIPTS	Cash sales														
	Debtors														
	Other receipts														
	Loan received														
	TOTAL RECEIPTS														
PAYMENTS	Purchases														
	Wages/salaries														
	NI														
	Rent														
	Rates														
	Insurance														
	Heat, light, power														
	Hire/lease														
	Printing/stationery														
	Postage/phone														
	Vehicle running														
	Fees (prof/legal)														
	Advertising														
	Interest (OD/loan)														
	Repayment (loan)														
	Capital payments														
	Other (VAT etc)														
	TOTAL PAYMENTS														
Net inflow (outflow)															
Opening cash book balance b/f															
Closing cash book balance															
Budget															

197

Appendix 9

Short-term Cash Forecast

Rolling four-weekly cash requisition

£000	Actual W/E 24 April	Projection — Week ending 1 May	8 May	15 May	22 May
Income					
Sales ledger	85.5	200.0	60.0	50.0	40.0
Other	—	—	—	—	—
Subtotal	85.5	200.0	60.0	50.0	40.0
Expenditure					
Wages	6.1	7.0	7.0	7.0	7.0
Salaries	13.4	—	—	—	13.5
Inland revenue	—	21.2	—	—	—
Standing orders	—	12.4	—	—	—
Sundries	0.9	1.0	1.0	1.0	1.0
Purchase Ledger	—	25.0	—	30.0	—
A)	15.1	—	18.9	—	19.1
B)	7.8				
C) (these are	11.6				
D) individual	5.5				
E) suppliers by	5.8				
F) name)		70.0			
G)			46.0		
Hire purchase	1.1				
Subtotal	67.3	136.6	72.0	38.0	40.6
Balance in week	18.2	63.4	(12.9)	12.0	(0.6)
Bank balance b/f	(272.0)	(253.8)	(190.4)	(203.3)	(191.3)
c/f	(253.8)	(190.4)	(203.3)	(191.3)	(191.9)
Average for W/E					
24 April Last week's					
(265) forecast	(138.7)	(185.3)	(198.2)	(196.2)	—
Creditor analysis					
Current	232.3	211.1	277.4	277.4	252.4
Overdue one month	162.0	152.5	98.7	98.7	93.7
two months	34.0	18.9	131.3	85.3	85.3
three months +	—	—	18.9	—	—
Opening balance	428.3	382.5	526.3	461.4	431.4
Purchases	—	238.8	—	—	—
Subtotal	428.3	621.5	526.3	461.4	431.4
Payments	45.8	95.0	64.9	30.0	19.1
Closing balance	382.5	526.3	461.4	431.4	412.3
Last week's forecast	382.5	526.3	461.4	431.4	—

Illustrative Routine Reports

Daily/Weekly

- Cash position
- Orders by products/activities
- Sales by products/activities
- Stock on hand
- Out of stock items
- Order backlog by products/activities
- Overdue deliveries inwards
- Factory reject ratio by product

Monthly

- Profit and loss accounts
- Order analysis by product
- Sales analysis by product
- Stock by product
- Balance sheet
- Order backlog by product and gross margin
- Debtors analysed by age/days outstanding
- Creditors analysed by age/days credit
- Cash flow
- Budget variance analysis and causes

Quarterly

- Review and reprojection of plans
- R & D progress report

Performance Summary

Appendix 11a

Company		Period	
		Date of issue	

P&L — £000

P&L	To date			Year end		
	ACT	P2	BUD	P2	BUD	L/Y
Orders						
GM %						
Net revenue						
Gross margin (GM)						
Selling						
Marketing						
G&A						
R&D						
General overhead						
Trading profit						
Grants & other income						
Operating profit						
Corporate						
Depreciation						
Interest						
Profit before tax						
PBT – last year						
Ratios to revenue						
GM %						
Overhead %						
PBT %						
ATO						

STATISTICS

STATISTICS	At period end		
	ACT	P2	BUD
Backlog shippable this F/Y			
Service run rate this F/Y			
Total backlog			
GM % in backlog			
Service run rate – annual			
GM % in SRR			
No of employees			
Temporary			
Period expense: average 3 mos fwd			
Break-even			
Stock (ex spares)			
Turns (3 periods fwd)			
Debtors			
Debtors days O/S			
Cash flow YTD			
PBT			
Depreciation			
Accruals & provisions			
Cash from operations			
Working capital in (out)			
Capital expenditure ( )			
Tax & dividends ( )			
Cash flow YTD			
Average NOA YTD			

Notes: (1) NOA = Net operating assets (3) P2 = Assumed profit (5) L/Y = Last year
(2) Service = Contracts for reprojection at end Q2 (6) YTD = Year to date
maintenance etc (4) F/Y = Financial year

Appendix 11b # Key Trends

£000

Period 10

	1	2	3	4	5	6	7	8	9	10	11	12	13	YTD	Basis
Revenues	895	1098												18,800	YTD
PBT	−361	−301												900	YTD
NOA 3743	5566	5404	7012											6,800	AVE
Cash balance	258	−47	−1354											−700	AVE
Cash flow 2434	−2184	−297	−1307											−4,150	YTD
ROR %	−40	−27	7	−10											YTD
ATO	2.50	2.60	4.28	2.83										etc	YTE
ROI %	−101	−71	30	−20											YTE
Orders	336	2412	789	554	840										YTD
Backlog	5875	7525	6611	6034	5727										AVE
Orders/revenue	0.58	3.17	0.46	0.49	0.73										YTD
Per expense	766	769	901	773	984	983									YTC
Break-even revenue	1693	1804	1765	1915	2051	1798									YTD
Head count	686	684	608	620	637	653									YTD
Gross manuf. stock	3855	4121	4292	4303	4512	4247	4431								AVE
Stock turns	2.07	2.09	2.14	2.37	2.43	2.42	2.23								AVE
Debtors	5450	4399	5693	5253	4221	5933	4993	4119							AVE
Debtors days	60	70	90	97	67	70	49	61							AVE
Creditors	1929	1294	1772	1865	1971	1615	1656	1807	1976						AVE
Creditors days	55	70	71	50	61	53	47	47	60						AVE

(FIGURES OMITTED)

Note: ATO = Asset turnover
AVE = Average
ROI = Return on investment
ROR = Return on revenue
YTD = Year to date

Monthly Reporting Format

The following six schedules are used by a trading company as monthly management reports. The principles are more important than the details, which can be adapted to any business.

Schedule 1: Key information

	Period		Cumulative − periods			Full year		
	Budget	*Actual*	*Budget*	*Projec-tion*	*Actual*	*Last year*	*Budget*	*Projec-tion*
	a	b	c	d	e	f	g	h
1. Net profit								
Net profit/sales %								
Gross margin/sales %								
Net profit/capital employed %								
2. Cash flow in (out)								
Current ratio								
Liquidity ratio								
Age of debtors (days)								
Age of creditors (days)								
3. Orders received								
Order backlog								
4. Number of employees								
Revenue per employee								
Profit per employee (annualised)								
5. Turnover of NOA								

Notes: (i) Latest projection will be identified by number or date.
 (ii) Substitute latest projection for budget in column (a) when appropriate.
 (iii) Some of the ratios used in this report are referred to in Chapter 3.

Schedule 2: Profit summary as at (date)

Period	Budget a	Latest projection b	Actual c
1			
2			
3			
4			
5			
6			
7			
8			
To date see note (i)	————	————————	————
9			
10			
11			
12			
13			
Year	————	————————	————
Previous projections see note (ii) at			
at		————————	
		————————	

Notes: (i) Subtotal to end of current period to give the cumulative profit.

(ii) These figures show the trend of management views during the progress of the year.

Schedule 3: Summarised trading results at period . . . for the . . . months ended (date)

| This month | | | Description | Cumulative | | | | | | Annual | | |
| Actual £ | % | Variance £ | | Actual £ | % | Budget £ | Reprojection £ | Last year £ | % | Budget £ | Reprojection £ | Last year £ |
						Variance						
			Detailed results in supporting schedule for each main subtotal.									

Schedule 4: Balance sheet as at (date)

Description	Month end		Year end	
	Actual	*Plan*	*Actual* *Last year*	*Forecast* *Current*
Fixed				

Current assets
  Stocks
  Debtors
  Cash				

Current liabilities
  Creditors
  Tax				

Net Current				
Other				
ASSETS EMPLOYED				

Source of funds
  Share capital
  Revenue reserves
    Current year
    Previous years				

SHAREHOLDERS' FUNDS Loans				

Schedule 5: Funds flow for the period to (date)

	Current month		Cum. to date		Annual forecast
	Actual	Variance	Actual	Variance	
A. SOURCE					
Self-generated					
Profit					
Depreciation					
Other					
TOTAL CASH IN					
B. APPLICATION					
Changes in working					
capital increase					
(decrease)					
Deposits					
Debtors					
Stocks					
Creditors					
Subtotal					
Net capital expenditure					
Subtotal					
Other					
C. MOVEMENT IN					
LIQUIDITY					
Cash and bank					
(ie A − B)					

Schedule 6: Order state as at (date)

PART I

	This month GM %	Latest projection GM %	This year	Budget	Latest projection
			Cumulative to date		
Order backlog at beginning					
Orders received					
Orders despatched					
Order backlog at end (see Part II)					

PART II
Forecast of delivery programme

Next month
Following month
Thereafter

Total of backlog at
period end as above

PART III
Trend of orders

Period — see note (i)	Amount	Budget	Latest projection
Q1			
Q2			
P7			
etc			
Total to date as above			

Notes: (i) For the current quarter, show by periods.
(ii) Orders will need analysis separately by product.

Appendix 11d

Examples of Report Presentation

The forms of reporting contained here are used by a financial controller for visual presentation to the board.

1. Orders
2. Revenues
3. Gross margin %
4. Period expense
5. Cash

Chart 1: Orders (cumulative)

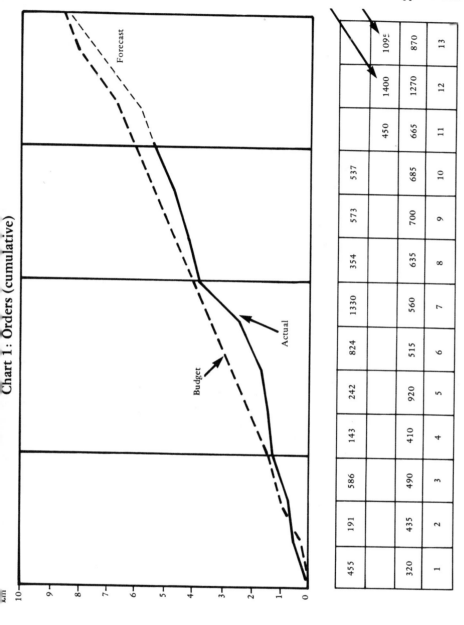

| | Actual | Budget | Forecast |

PERIOD	ACTUAL	FORECAST	BUDGET
1	455		320
2	191		435
3	586		490
4	143		410
5	242		920
6	824		515
7	1330		560
8	354		635
9	573		700
10	537		685
11		450	665
12		1400	1270
13		1095	870

£000 average	
YEAR	
BUDGET	8475
FORECAST	8180
ACTUAL	5235

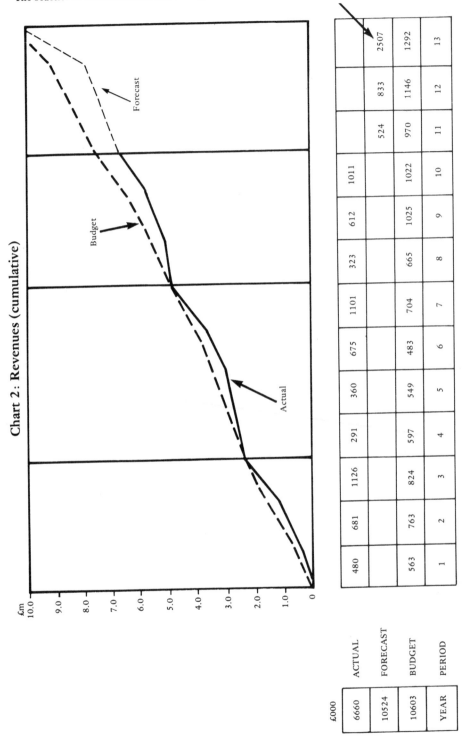

Chart 2: Revenues (cumulative)

	1	2	3	4	5	6	7	8	9	10	11	12	13
ACTUAL	480	681	1126	291	360	675	1101	323	612	1011	524	833	2507
FORECAST													1292
BUDGET	563	763	824	597	549	483	704	665	1025	1022	970	1146	1292
PERIOD	1	2	3	4	5	6	7	8	9	10	11	12	13

£000	
6660	ACTUAL
10524	FORECAST
10603	BUDGET
	YEAR

Chart 3 : Gross margin %

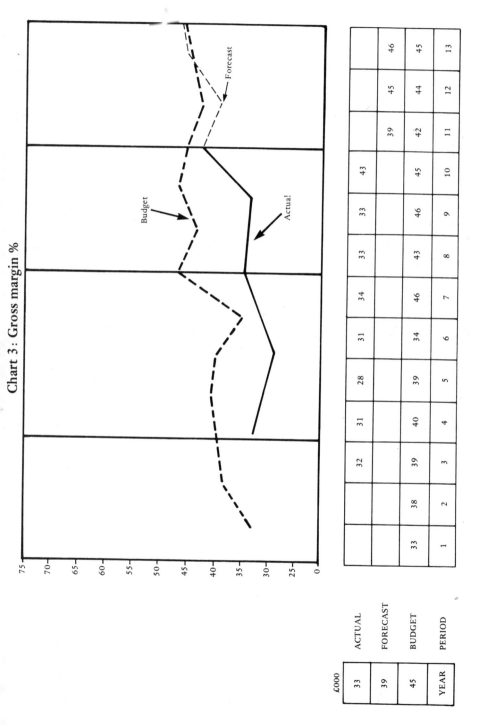

ACTUAL	33			32	31	28	31	34	33	33	43		
FORECAST	39		38	39	40	39	34	46	43	46	45	39	45	46
BUDGET	45											42	44	45
PERIOD	YEAR	1	2	3	4	5	6	7	8	9	10	11	12	13

£000

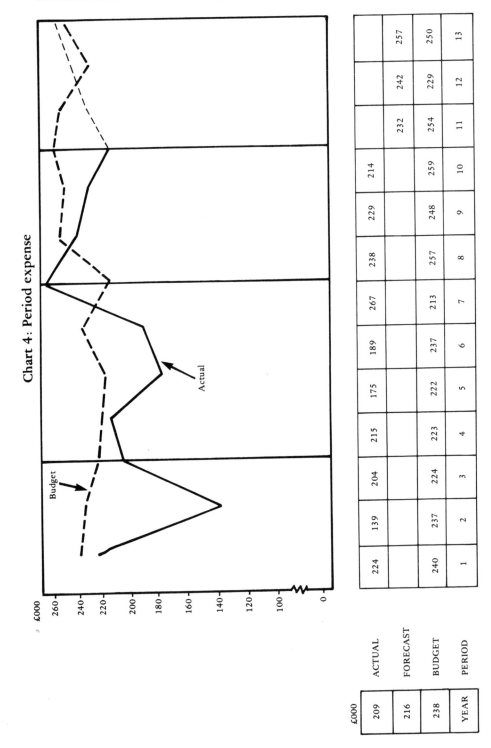

Chart 4: Period expense

£000															
	224	139	204	215	175	189	267	238	229	214		232	242	257	ACTUAL
209															
															FORECAST
216															
	240	237	224	223	222	237	213	257	248	259	254	229	250	BUDGET
238															
£000	1	2	3	4	5	6	7	8	9	10	11	12	13	PERIOD
YEAR															

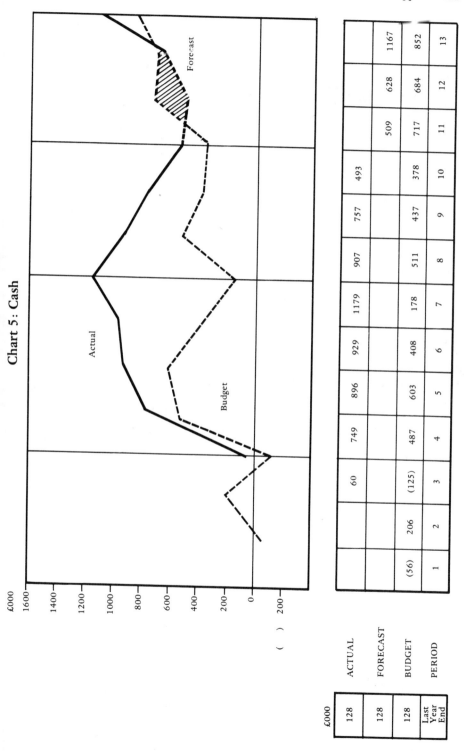

Chart 5 : Cash

£000: 1600 1400 1200 1000 800 600 400 200 0 ( ) 200

Actual

Forecast

Budget

	ACTUAL	FORECAST	BUDGET	PERIOD
	(56)			1
	206			2
	60		(125)	3
	749		487	4
	896		603	5
	929		408	6
	1179		178	7
	907		511	8
	757		437	9
	493		378	10
		509	717	11
		628	684	12
		1167	852	13

£000	
ACTUAL	128
FORECAST	128
BUDGET	128
	Last Year End

Example of a Key Ratio Summary in a Consumer Credit Business

Key Ratios	Jan	Feb	Mar	*Apr	May	Jun	Jul	Aug	Sep	Oct	Nov	Dec	Jan	Feb	Mar	Total year
A. *New Business*																
Number of new accounts																
Actual value of new accounts (£000)																
Budget value of new accounts (£000)																
Reproject value of new accounts (£000) (i)																
Average new loan																
Further advance																
B. *Gross Margin*																
Actual % (iii)																
Budget % (ii)																
C. *Advertising*																
Cost per £100 of new loans																
Cost per new a/c																
Budget (ii)																
D. *Underwriting*																
Cost per £100 of new loans																
Cost per new a/c																
Budget (ii)																
E. *Accounting and Administration*																
Cost per £100 of balances																
Cost per account																
Budget (ii)																
F. *Credit Control*																
Cost per £100 of balances																
Cost per account																
Budget (ii)																
G. *Loan balances (£000)*																
Actual																
Budget																
Reprojected value of balances (i)																

Notes: (i) Reprojected at end each quarter.
(ii) Displaced when reprojected to the revised forecast.
(iii) Income less cost of money.
*Year end.

215

Value Added Statement

for the year ended ——— 198-

	Current year		Preceding year	
	£	%	£	%
Turnover				
Less: Bought-in materials and services				
Depreciation	————		————	
Value added		100.00		100.00
Applied as follows:				
Employees' (remuneration, pensions, NHI, etc)				
Interest on borrowings				
Government taxes				
Shareholder (dividends)	————	————	————	————
Total applied				
Retained for development	————	————	————	————
TOTAL		100.00		100.00
Value added per employee	£ ═══		£ ═══	

Note: Bonus arrangements can be made in relation to employee improvements in productivity as reflected by the employee percentage of value added. Such schemes have the great advantage of improving communications within the company, and encouraging greater interest in the results on the part of all employees.

Job Description Format

1. *Job title*

2. *Reports to*

3. *General description of task*
   This provides an overall summary of the main responsibilities attaching to the job.

4. *Detailed tasks*
   Main responsibilities broken down into appropriate sub-tasks.

5. *Works closely with*
   This shows the relationships with the other employees.

6. *Limitation on authority*
   This details the restrictions, financial or otherwise, attaching to the job.

7. *Key performance criteria*
   This highlights those criteria by which proper performance of the job may be judged.

Date

Appendix 14

Some Aspects of Employment Conditions

Legislation

The principal legislation affecting employment is to be found in the Employment Protection (Consolidation) Act 1978 (EPCA). In addition, the following are relevant:

Health and Safety at Work Act 1974 (HASAWA)
Sex Discrimination Act 1975 (SDA)
Equal Pay Act 1970 (EPA)
Race Relations Act 1976 (RRA)
Social Security and Housing Benefits Act 1982 (SSHBA)
The Employment Acts 1980 and 1982 (EA)
Trade Union and Labour Relations Act 1974 (TULRA)

Recruitment and selection

In essence, by virtue of the RRA and SDA it is unlawful for the employer to discriminate in the search for employees or their selection on the grounds of race or sex. There are some very limited exceptions.

Contract

While this is essentially a contract to which the general principles of common law apply, this freedom is significantly restricted by the several acts of Parliament which directly bear on employment matters, as well as trade custom and, in the case of recognised trade unions, collective agreements and rules.

Apart from the normal remedies open to an injured party, the statutory law gives employees the right to seek redress through an industrial tribunal.

A contract may be oral or in writing, but in employment matters, a written agreement is obviously essential.

Under the EPCA, the employee is required to provide an employee, within 13 weeks of the commencement of employment, with a written statement setting out specified terms of the employment. Although frequently referred to as a contract, it does not technically have that legal status (see p118).

Pay

The employee is entitled to an itemised pay statement. The EPCA legislates for:

— guaranteed payments
— lay off

— medical absence
— maternity leave —
time off for trade union duties. (An ACAS code of practice refers.)

Wages have to be paid in cash or by cheque. Agreement will be required to pay monthly and by bank transfer.

Duties

The employee's duties should be clearly and carefully defined in the contract. In addition to the agreed terms, the following are implied:

Employer (i) to indemnify employees in respect of losses incurred in the course of employment
          (ii) to provide safe working conditions
Employee (i) to work with reasonable competence
          (ii) to obey reasonable instructions
          (iii) not to make secret profits
          (iv) not to disclose employer's confidential information.

Notice period

An employee is entitled as a minimum to the following periods of notice:

Service	Notice
1 month or less	None
1 month to 2 years	1 week
2 years	2 weeks

Thereafter one additional week for each additional year of service with a maximum of 12.

An employee who has worked for at least four weeks is required to give one week's notice.

Terms of the employment contract may extend these minimum requirements.

Termination

Dismissal is brought about by the termination of an employee's contract by the employer.

Constructive dismissal is deemed to have taken place when an employee is forced to terminate the contract because the employer in a material way unilaterally breaks, or proposes to break, the contract.

Justification for dismissal

(a) lack of capability
(b) unsatisfactory conduct
(c) redundancy
(d) failure to join a trade union in certain specific situations concerning union membership in that company and adherence to the correct procedures.
(e) frustration by illegality
(f) a limited number of other grounds dependent upon the test of 'reasonable under the circumstances'.

Wages may be paid in lieu of notice.

Unfair dismissal

If dismissal cannot be justified it is deemed to be 'unfair'.

Employees have a right not to be unfairly dismissed provided they have completed one year's service (extended to two years in the case of companies with 20 or fewer employees).

There are also exceptions in connection with employees over retiring age and those who were engaged on fixed term contracts.

It is open to an employee who considers that he has been unfairly dismissed to complain to an industrial tribunal within three months of receiving dismissal notice.

Redundancy

Redundancy occurs when the services of employees are dispensed with because:

- the employer ceases, or intends to cease, business
- the employer intends to reduce the number of employees.

An employee may require redundancy payment if:

- he has been laid off or kept on short-time without pay for four consecutive weeks (or for a broken series of at least six weeks in a period of 13), and
- there is no reasonable prospect that normal working will be resumed.

An employee is eligible for redundancy payment if:

- he has completed two years' continuous service since reaching the age of 18
- he works for 16 hours or more per week (or eight hours or more where the employment has been for five or more years with the 'same' employer).

He is not entitled to redundancy if:

- he accepts alternative employment
- he unreasonably refuses an offer of a new employment on the same terms by the same employer.
- he unreasonably refuses when offered different duties at a different location and there has been a reasonable trial period of not less than four weeks.

The minimum amount of statutory redundancy payment is calculated for employees aged 41–65 (60 women) at the rate of one and a half weeks' pay with a maximum of £145 per week for each year of service with a maximum of 20 years (the basic rate).

The basic rate is reduced for age as follows:

22 to 40 years	at the rate of 1 week's pay
18 to 21 years	at the rate of half week's pay
Over 64 (59 women)	Basic rate discounted by the number of months in excess of 65 (60 women) as a ratio of 12.

The employer is currently entitled to reclaim 35 per cent of the statutory redundancy payment from the government, provided the necessary procedures are correctly followed.

There are statutory procedures for notifying recognised trade unions if 100 or more employees at any one establishment are to be dismissed.

Consultation

In the case of companies employing more than 250 people, the 1982 Employment Act requires a statement in the annual directors' report concerning the arrangements in force for informing, consulting and involving employees in the business of the company.

Health and Safety

The HASAWA 1974 places on the employer the duty to ensure, so far as is reasonably practicable, the health, safety and welfare of employees while they are at work and requires the employer to publish the policy concerning safety and ensure implementation by adequate instruction and training.

The following are particularly affected:

- plant and equipment
- handling, storage and transport
- premises.

Other relevant legislation:

- The Factories Act 1961
- The Fire Precautions Act 1971
- The Offices, Shops and Railways Premises Act 1963.

There is a statutory requirement to:

- report immediately any fatality, major injury or dangerous occurrence
- keep records of accidents involving incapacity for more than three days
- provide alternative means of escape when there are 10 employees or more above ground floor (20 at ground level)
- provide 40 square feet of office space per employee (and not less than 400 cubic feet).

Example of an Appraisal Testing Report

Extract from a psychological appraisal report on an applicant for the position of general manager in a large food company.

On tests of verbal and numerical reasoning ability, Mr Y obtained respectively Superior and Very Superior results surpassing 85% and 96% of the English adult population.

The above results combined with his previous experience suggest that he should be capable of meeting the problem solving requirements of an appointment such as the one under consideration.

Temperament

The temperament indication suggests strong self-control, self-reliance and amenability, ethical attitudes, straightforwardness, cheerfulness, caution in judgements and decision making, tact in interpersonal relationships and steadfast ambition.

He should maintain sound control over his emotions and feelings. Will fit in well with others. He likes to work to his own standards, and can bring a constructive and creative imagination to his responsibilities. He sets himself high personal standards of performance and is able to work persistently in the maintenance of such standards. He tends also to expect high standards of other people.

His major assets are his strong need to organise, analyse and communicate the results of his problems.

His major deficits are that he finds it difficult to deal with incompetent individuals who hate making decisions.

Conclusions

Mr Y is well qualified intellectually and temperamentally for the position and should be considered seriously for the appointment.

(By courtesy of Elizabeth Collier Assessments)

Appendix 16

Computer Procedures and Guidance Notes

Part I: The development of in-house capability
Guidelines for controlling computer projects

1. Get the project off to the right start:

   - importance of User Executive and a full-time Project Manager
   - Project Manager technically and managerially competent (track record)
   - resist temptation to force computer people to be over-optimistic (ie listen for the truth, not what you want to hear).

2. Importance of good methods:

   - systems and programming standards
   - staged approach to project development
   - project management methods and reporting
   - all projects have signed terms of reference (signed by Users not Systems).

3. Allow proper time for the survey stage (KEY):

   - only authorise the survey at the start (ie do not authorise the whole project until you know what you are in for)
   - ensure the business problem to be solved is identified correctly and the problem boundaries (problem identification before problem solution)
   - ensure more than one alternative solution is evaluated (ie mainframe, mini, micro, calculator, pencil and paper, packages). Ensure you understand why the chosen solution has been recommended and that it looks sensible and up-to-date (without being avant garde).

4. Ensure all potential users are involved:

   - failure to involve users will lead to problems
   - this is especially true as minis move to the workplace as part of the operational system.

5. Allow proper time for evaluation stage and decision (KEY):

   - very important decision point — once crossed, the project is on the launch pad
   - the decision may be a rejection on grounds of cost, time or unsatisfactory result.

6. Identify the changing role of the user during project development:

   - survey report: strategic decisions on hardware selection and location
   - functional description (business specification): tactical and management decisions on how it will work

Note: The functional description is véry important.
All key outputs approved by users will be included.

— systems specification: detailed operating decisions
— programs: no user role
— computer appreciation courses are of limited value — make sure the technicians express themselves in user and business terms (or get better technicians)
— require regular reports on progress.

7. Insist on thorough testing and implementation planning:

— after systems testing comes user acceptance testing, volume testing and data testing
— some form of parallel running is mandatory
— think through changes in the user organisation and make them in good time
— implement one step at a time.

8. Bear in mind that 'flexibility' has to be built into computer systems — it does not happen naturally. Few problems are easier than they appear at first sight and it is worth taking a little longer at the start to avoid confusion and duplication later.

Note: 'User' here refers to different people. As the project develops it will involve lower levels of management. At the survey stage it will probably be the general manager or managing director.

The importance of project management cannot be over emphasised. Of all the risk factors, weakness in project management is most likely to lead to problems in any computer development project.

Part II: Guidance notes for controlling the ongoing running and maintenance of computer systems

1. Recognise the need for documented procedures:

— reliable operation depends on soundly constructed procedures which are 'idiot-proof' and change rarely
— formalise run requests for all jobs both routine and ad hoc
— take extra care at times of change
— establish communication channels between user departments and operations staff.

2. Recover rapidly from any failure:

— hardware fault location and engineer call-out
— back-up copies of all data files, programs and job control must exist with copies stored off-site
— test re-running and recover after a failure.

3. Take precautions against a 'disaster' (about three occur each year in UK computer rooms):

— precautions against physical risks
— disaster planning
— disaster testing.

4. Control system amendment requests:
   - ensure correct authorisation
   - program testing and release procedures
   - control of maintenance workload (analyse monthly: jobs completed, jobs in progress, jobs not yet started, new jobs this month).

5. Aim to localise operations rather than processing everything on one central monster.

Appendix 17

Corporation Tax Computation

for the accounting year ended _____ 198-

(The numbers on the left-hand margin refer to the explanatory notes on page 227.)

Schedule D, Case I (Trading Profit)	£	£
Net profit, before tax, as shown by the accounts		xxx
Add:		
1. Depreciation	xx	
2. Subscriptions & donations disallowable	xx	
3. Legal & professional charges disallowable	xx	
4. Entertaining expenses disallowable	xx	
5. General bad debt provision	xx	
6. Losses on disposal of fixed assets	xx	
7. Capital expenditure charged to revenue	xx	xxx
		xxx
Deduct:		
8. Dividends from UK companies	xx	
9. Dividends from overseas companies	xx	
10. Rents received (net)	xx	
11. Profit on disposal of fixed assets	xx	
12. Expenditure charged to reserves	xx	xxx
		xxx
13. Capital allowances		xxx
Profit assessable under Case I		xxx
14. Less: Trading losses brought forward		xxx
		xxx
15. Add: Profits from property assessed under Schedule A	xx	
16. Untaxed interest assessed under Schedule D Case III	xx	
17. Overseas income assessed under Schedule D Case IV or V	xx	
		xxx
		xxx
18. Chargeable gains	xx	
19. Less: capital losses	xx	xxx
Profits chargeable to corporation tax		xxx
Taxation payable calculated at CT rate		xx
Less: advance corporation tax paid		xx
Corporation tax remaining to be paid		xx

Explanatory notes

1. Added back because company depreciation practice is ignored (tax relief being given through capital allowances).

2. Most subscriptions and donations are deemed to be expenditure incurred 'not wholly and exclusively for the purposes of the trade'.

3. Many legal and professional charges are allowable. Those disallowed and added back relate to expenditure deemed to be of a capital nature, such as in connection with asset purchase or with capital raising.

4. Expenditure incurred on entertaining UK customers is not allowed as a charge for tax purposes.

5. Provisions made against specific debts are allowable.
   Provisions of a general nature are not.

6. As in note (1), company practice is ignored.

7. Added back because capital expenditure is not allowable as a charge against income.

8. Dividends are deducted because they have borne tax at the time of payment, known as 'franked investment income'.

9. Overseas dividends are received after suffering overseas tax and UK taxation. They are therefore excluded.

10. Net rents received (ie gross rents less allowable expenses) are taxed under Schedule A and are therefore excluded from Schedule D.

11. Excluded for the same reason as in note (6).

12. The fact that trading expenses may be charged in the accounts against a reserve account does not prevent them being allowable for tax purposes. Similarly, there may be relief for expenditure classified in the accounts as 'extraordinary'.

13. Capital allowances comprise both first-year and annual allowances and are the method used by the Inland Revenue to depreciate assets.

14. Trading losses as calculated for tax purposes may be relieved broadly as follows:
    – against other income in the period
    – carried back (usually for one year) to a previous period
    – carried forward against profits of the same trade.

15. See note (10)

16. Interest received gross is assessed under the rules applicable to Case III of Schedule D.

17. Overseas income is assessed under the rules applicable to Case IV of Schedule D in the case of 'securities' and Case V in the case of 'possessions'.

18. A chargeable gain arises when the asset is sold for a price in excess of the cost (as adjusted for tax purposes). The gain is reduced by a fraction, the effect of which is to charge capital gains at 30%.

19. Capital losses are computed in the same manner as gains, but may be relieved only against capital gains in the same or subsequent period.

Appendix 18

Capital Allowances

	First year		*Subsequent years*
1. Plant and machinery	Pre 14/3/84	100%)	
	14/3/84 − 31/3/85	75%)	25% on the reducing
	1/4/85 − 31/3/86	50%)	balance
	Thereafter nil		
2. Motor vehicles (private)	25%		25%
3. Motor vehicles (goods or for use in hiring)	As for plant and machinery		
4. Plant and machinery under HP	As for plant and machinery in relation to the capital element when the plant is brought into use		
5. Machinery leased	Nil		
	Note: The rental payments are allowed as an expense		
6. Industrial Buildings (at least 75 per cent used for a qualifying purpose) including additions and improvements	Pre 14/3/84	75%)	4%
	14/3/84 − 31/3/85	50%)	Also allowed for first
	1/4/85 − 31/3/86	25%)	year
	Thereafter nil		
Note: If located in Enterprise Zones (including shops, offices and hotels)	100%		
7. Hotel buildings	Pre 1/4/86 20%		4%
	Thereafter nil		Also allowed for first year
8. Scientific research expenditure	100%		
9. Patents	Nil		25% of the reducing balance from 1 April 1986 (previously 1/17 each year)

	First year	*Subsequent years*
10. Know-how	Nil	25% of the reducing balance from 1 April 1986 (previously 1/6 each year)

Index

tax assessments 121
tax credit 159
tax evasion 157
tax implications 122-3
tax liability 157
tax planning 157, 158
tax provisions 123
tax rates 158
taxation 142, 157-63
  basis of 159
technical plan 77-8, 183
technical progress 77
telephone operator 165
telephone usage 165
termination costs 54
terms of reference 166
third party claims 148
time and motion study 124
timescale 63
title reservation by seller 137-8
top-down planning 65, 66
total assets 46
trade creditors 101-2
trade debtors 99-101
Trade Descriptions Acts 1968 and 1972: 142
trade marks 144
trade unions 25, 114, 171
trading losses 160-61
trading results 204

Trading Standards Consumer Protection 139
trading terms 100
training 117
Truck Acts 119
true and fair view 37

ultra vires rule 134
under-capitalisation 60
Unfair Contracts Terms Act 1977: 137, 138
Unlisted Securities Market 38, 60
Unsolicited Goods and Services Act 1971: 140-41

value added statement 107-8, 216
value added tax (VAT) 162-3
variable costs 48-9
venture capital 23, 57, 58
visual aids 33

warranty 136
'what if' questions 66, 130
work improvement performance 124-5
work measurement 91
work study 124
working capital 46, 61, 99, 102, 103

year-end hockey stick 108-9